Easy-to-Make
Antique Furniture Reproductions

15 Small Projects

John A. Nelson

Photographs by Dr. Robert S. Fay
and Deborah Porter

Dover Publications, Inc., New York

To Julie

Copyright © 1982 by Van Nostrand Reinhold Company, Inc.
All rights reserved under Pan American and International Copyright Conventions.

Published in Canada by General Publishing Company, Ltd., 30 Lesmill Road, Don Mills, Toronto, Ontario.
Published in the United Kingdom by Constable and Company, Ltd.

This Dover edition, first published in 1988, is an unabridged republication of the work originally published by Van Nostrand Reinhold Company, New York, in 1982 under the title *Antique Furniture Reproduction: 15 Easy Projects*. The list of supplies at the end of the book has been updated for the present edition.

Manufactured in the United States of America
Dover Publications, Inc., 31 East 2nd Street, Mineola, N.Y. 11501

Library of Congress Cataloging-in-Publication Data

Nelson, John A., 1935–
    Easy-to-make antique furniture reproductions : 15 small projects / John A. Nelson ; photographs by Robert S. Fay and Deborah Porter.
        p.   cm.
    Rev. ed. of: Antique furniture reproduction.
    Bibliography: p.
    Includes index.
    ISBN 0-486-25671-5
    1. Furniture   making—Amateurs'   manuals.
I. Nelson, John A., 1935–   Antique furniture reproduction.   II. Title.
TT195.N44   1988
749'.1'0287—dc19   88-357
                                            CIP

Contents

Introduction 5

Notes for the Woodworker 6
Wood 6
Accessories 7
Tools 7
General Instructions 11
Detail and Assembly Drawings 11
Finishing Points 13

Eighteenth-Century Footstool 14
Shaker Candleholder 20
Three-Rail Towel Rack 26
Silverware Tray 30
"Lollipop" Candle Box 36
Shaker Drying Rack 42
Chippendale Mirror Frame 48
Three-Shelf Wall Rack 54
Eighteenth-Century Pipe Holder 60
Pennsylvania Dutch Child's Bench 70
Six-Board Blanket Chest 78
Standing Cupboard 86
Adjustable Candle Stand 94
Hanging Book Shelf With Drawers 102
Heirloom Watch Stand 112

Supplies 122

Index 127

Introduction

In terms of "style," nothing can quite compare with Early American furniture. This furniture is part of our heritage. To locate and purchase authentic, original pieces left behind by past American craftsmen, however, is both difficult and expensive. A solution that is easier than you might think, and certainly a satisfying one, is to acquire your own collection of Early American furniture by reproducing the pieces yourself.

This text has been written for the prospective woodworker who has never attempted any type of woodworking before. These projects naturally lend themselves to the home woodworker; they have that "handmade," "original" look not unlike the authentic Early American furniture of yesteryear. To benefit the beginner, detail drawings of each part, as well as thorough instructions for making each part and assembling the project, are provided. The dimensioned, detailed drawings alone will be most helpful to the more advanced wood shop enthusiast, especially if he would like to mass-produce any of the projects. Only basic hand tools are needed, which further helps the prospective woodworker to get started in the world of wood. Those with power tools will find the projects even simpler to complete.

That same feeling of personal satisfaction felt by the early craftsmen, accompanied by a certain closeness to history, will be experienced by the woodworker working on these projects. All fifteen projects were taken directly from an original antique. Each is simple to build—even for the novice—and, the cost of each project is nominal even when you take the high price of wood into account. There is one high cost factor, though, and that is time. But, for those who share a love for Early American furniture and accessories it is impossible to put a price on the satisfaction derived from making even the simplest of these projects.

Notes for the Woodworker

Whether you are an experienced woodworker or a novice, it is a good idea to read the following section before you begin your first project.

WOOD

There are two general classifications of wood—hardwood and softwood. Although most softwoods are softer than hardwoods, the terms hardwood and softwood do not refer to density, but rather to botanical origin. Most softwoods are evergreens; most hardwoods are from trees that shed their leaves in autumn. The term medium wood refers to wood that has the characteristics of both softwood and hardwood. Basically, medium wood is easier to work. In that respect it is similar to softwood, but it will look, feel, and finish like hardwood.

Common lumber is distinguished from the finish grades by a general coarseness of appearance, caused by various defects. #1 Common grade includes all sound, tight knots, with the size of the knot the determining factor in the grade. Very small pitch pockets, light stains, season checks, or equivalent characteristics are permitted. This grade is used for shelving and all uses where best quality and appearance of common lumber are required. #2 Common grade permits larger and more pronounced defects. #3 Common uses the lower cutting of the log and permissible characteristics are of a more pronounced nature than allowed in #2 common. #4 Common is much the same as #3 common, but defects are more extensive and more pronounced. #5 Common is the lowest recognized grade and allows all defects provided the piece is of usable quality. Most of the projects in this book call for common grade #2 or #3 pine wood in the materials lists. Pine is easy to work and it finishes nicely; #2 and #3 pine is usually very knotty, lower in price than clear #1 pine, and, if carefully selected, will have a lot more "character." If you would, however, rather use a different wood, the following is a list of good choices.

Note: The asterisks denote open-grained wood which is very porous and must be coated with a commercial wood filler before the final finishing process is begun.

SOFTWOOD
Basswood
Pine
Poplar
Red cedar
Redwood
Willow

MEDIUM WOOD
*Butternut
*Chestnut
Elm
Gum
*Limba
*Mahogony

HARDWOOD
*Ash
Birch
Cherry
Maple
*Oak
*Walnut

In colonial days three species of pine were used—Eastern (white) pine, Northern pitch (yellow) pine, and Southern hard (red) pine. Except for scrub trees along coastal Massachusetts, Rhode Island, and Long Island, the Northern pitch pine is almost extinct today. It was relatively hard with a pronounced grain and was used mostly for tabletops and the early cupboards and chest lids. Southern hard pine, strong with a pronounced grain, was used extensively in Virginia, the Carolinas, and Georgia. Often called "Pumpkin" pine, Eastern pine was used the most. It is very knotty and gives that authentic "old" look.

If possible, try to *choose* each board at the lumberyard. Look for straight wood that has "character" and interesting knots, but watch that knots are not on the edges of the board, as the knot could break away and ruin the finished project. When working with pine, try to construct each project in such a manner as to highlight any knots or interesting grain structure.

Lumber is designated by its rough size, not its finished size. A "2 by 4" is actually only 1¾ inches by 3¾ inches in size. Be sure you are getting a finished size that is large enough for each project. The following chart should help you in obtaining the correct finished sizes.

DESIGNATION	ACTUAL SIZE
1 by 2 inches	¾ by 1½ inches
1 by 3 inches	¾ by 2½ inches
1 by 4 inches	¾ by 3½ inches
1 by 6 inches	¾ by 5½ inches
1 by 8 inches	¾ by 7¼ inches
1 by 10 inches	¾ by 9¼ inches
1 by 12 inches	¾ by 11¼ inches

ACCESSORIES

The back of the book includes a list of some of the many vendors who manufacture or sell reproductions of many old accessories, such as latches, hinges, drawer pulls and the like. These will give your projects an authentic finished, antique look. Write for these catalogs to give you an idea exactly what products are available.

Antique-cut nails, for example, are a "must" for your projects. The Tremont Nail Company (listed under sources) sells a variety of nails that are exactly the same as the ones used over one hundred years ago.

TOOLS

An assortment of the most basic woodworking tools are all that is necessary to complete the projects presented in this book.

Crosscut saw (22 inches long, and 10 teeth per inch)
Jack plane (9 inches long or longer)
Try square
Plain bit brace *or* open gear hand drill with various size twist drills
Claw hammer
Nail set (1/16 inch size)
Coping saw
Sanding block
Tape measure or folding rule (6 feet long) (or folding extension rule)
Wood clamps (two or more)
Wood chisels (¼ inches wide and ½ inches wide)
Half round rasp
Screwdrivers of different sizes
Spokeshave

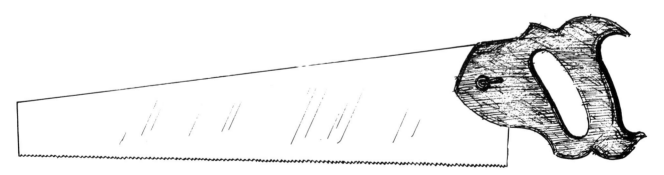

Crosscut Saw

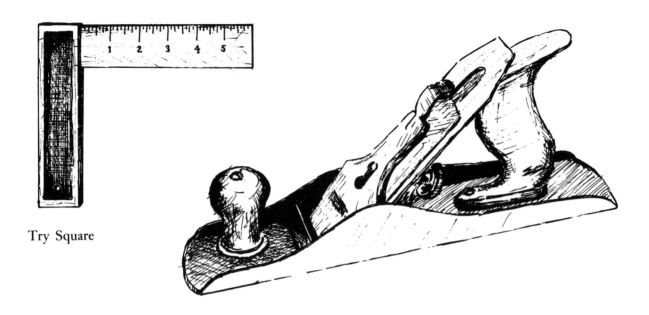

Try Square

Jack Plane

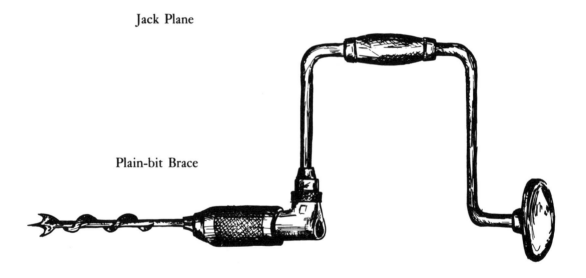

Plain-bit Brace

Open-gear Hand Drill

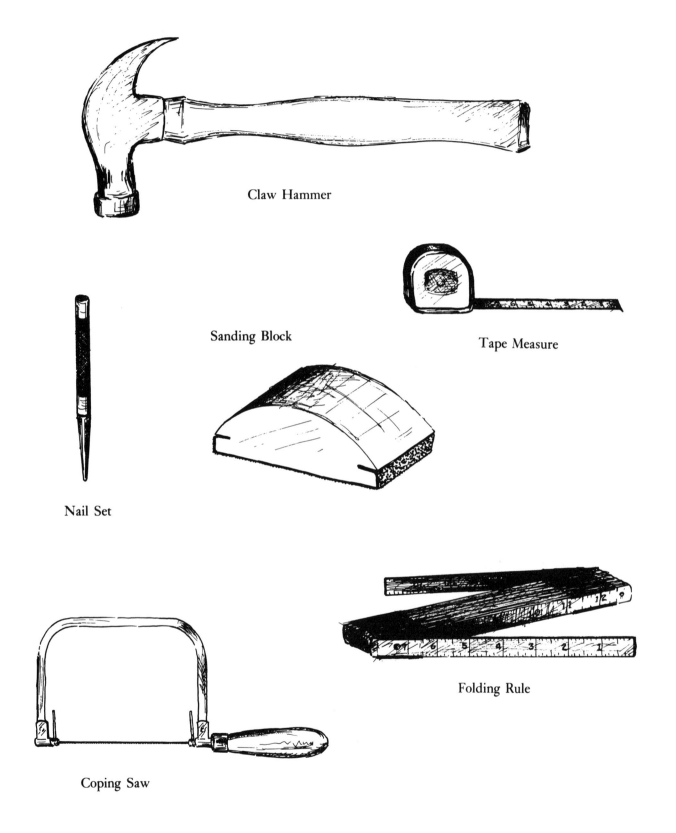

Claw Hammer

Sanding Block

Tape Measure

Nail Set

Coping Saw

Folding Rule

Some additional tools that would be helpful, but that are not essential, are the following:

Electric drill, ⅜ inch size
Saber saw
Table saw or radial-arm saw, 9-inch-diameter blade or larger
Drill press
Electric sander, 3½ inch by 9 inch plate
Router, ¾ horse power or more

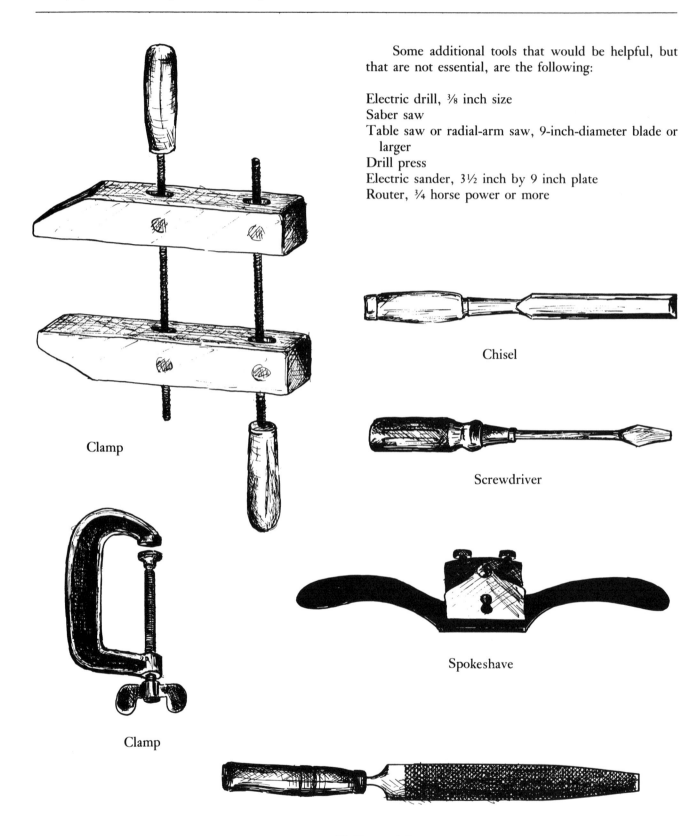

Clamp

Chisel

Screwdriver

Clamp

Spokeshave

Half-round Rasp

GENERAL INSTRUCTIONS

Within the category of "Early American," there are three general periods of time and styles of furniture, Pilgrim (from 1620 to about 1720), Colonial (from 1720 to about 1780), and Federal (from 1780 to about 1830). Most of the projects presented here would be placed in the early Colonial period.

The projects are presented in order of their complexity; that is, the easiest project comes first and the more complex problems appear toward the back of the book.

For each Project I recommend that the following simple suggestions be followed:

1. Carefully study the assembly drawing. Be sure you fully understand how the project is assembled before starting any work.
2. Purchase all material needed to complete the project. Hand pick the wood, if possible. Look for wood that is "interesting," meaning that it has knots and "character," and that it is straight.
3. Carefully make all measurements for cutting and draw all cutting lines using the "square" for perfect 90-degree angles of each cut. Use a scribe or sharp 4–H pencil for all lines.
4. Make each individual part according to the detail drawing. The beginning woodworker should read and follow all instructions carefully.
5. Before starting assembling, sand all parts smoothly.
6. Before assembling project, check that all parts fit together exactly.
7. Wipe all excess glue away with a damp rag before it hardens, as it cannot be scraped off after it dries and it shows through the finished stain. All glue must be removed before the stain is applied.
8. As you assemble each project, be sure each part is "flush," that is, tight fitting, and "square." Do not rush the final assembly process. Clamp all work tightly, if possible.

9. After assembly and before applying any stain, be sure all surfaces are perfectly smooth. The "distressing" process is explained in full in the instructions for finishing the first project. If you do choose to "distress" your projects, it should be done at this time. Be sure to resand after the distressing process. To add further to the distressing process, use a rasp, file or sandpaper on edges that would normally wear with use, to achieve that "worn" look.
10. After distressing and fine resanding is done, completely "rub down" the complete project using #0000 steel wool.
11. It is good practice to completely clean your work area and allow time for the dust to settle before starting the finishing process.
12. Before staining, wipe the complete project with a cloth that is slightly dampened with turpentine. All surfaces must be dust-free and thoroughly dry, before the stain is applied.

Note: The finishing process takes much more time than does the actual making of the project. Do not try to rush this part of the project.

DETAIL AND ASSEMBLY DRAWINGS

The detail drawings used in this text use the standard multi-view drawing system. If you do not understand how to read blueprints, take a few minutes to study the following illustrations. A multi-view drawing is a method used to fully represent an object so there will not be any question as to how it is to be made. A detail drawing can include one, two, three, or however many views are needed. The standard method is to start with the most important view and call it the "front view." If needed, a top view is added and/or a right side view. The illustration shows how a die appears to the eye.

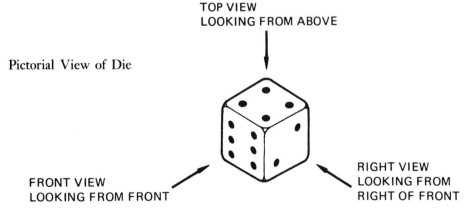

Pictorial View of Die

TOP VIEW
LOOKING FROM ABOVE

FRONT VIEW
LOOKING FROM FRONT

RIGHT VIEW
LOOKING FROM
RIGHT OF FRONT

This drawing shows how the die will look if you look *directly* at the front view.

Front View

If you look directly down at the die it will look like this.

Top View

If you go around to the right side and look at the die, it should look like this.

Right-side View

Think of the die being made of a piece of cardboard. As it unfolds, it will look like this.

The Die Unfolded

Completely flattened out, it will look like this.

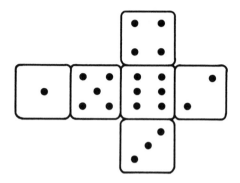

The Die Flattened Out

Now separated, the six sides will look like this.

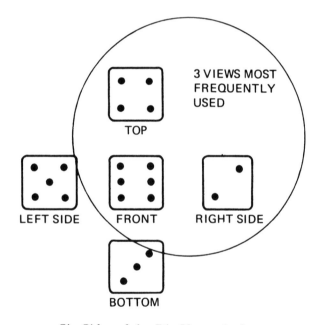

Six Sides of the Die Unattached

The views usually given in the following detail drawing of the projects are the front view, and right side view, although the bottom view and left side views are sometimes used, too. Notice how the top view is directly above the front view. Notice, also, how the right side view is directly to the right of the front view. This is the standard method used in industry to illustrate all parts manufactured.

An assembly drawing is similar to a detail drawing, but it usually does not have any dimensions and illustrates where the various parts are located and how the project goes together.

Refer to the first project—the Eighteenth-Century Footstool. On page 15 there is a pictorial drawing of the footstool or how it will look when completed. On page 17 there is an assembly drawing of the footstool with a front view and a right side view. Notice that there are five balloons with figures inside each. The figure inside each balloon corresponds to the detail drawing number of that part and where it is located in the overall assembly.

Example: The balloon with the number 1 in it (in front and right side view) indicates detail drawing 1, which is the ends of the stool. Drawing 1 is a detail drawing and fully illustrates exactly what part 1 should look like, when completed. The balloon with a number 2 in it indicates part 2, the two side braces. This indicates the shape and where the two side braces are located. Part numbers 3, 4, and 5 are also in balloons and have fully dimensioned detail drawings of each. All projects have an assembly drawing and fully dimensioned detailed drawing of each part. This will simplify making all parts and putting the assembly together.

Study all drawings before starting any project, in order to have a mental picture of exactly what must be done. You will avoid errors this way.

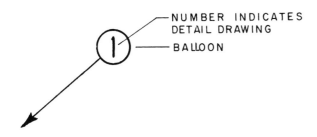

The Numbered Balloon Corresponds to the Detailed Drawing

FINISHING POINTS

Thorough instructions for finishing are provided with each project. You'll notice that some projects call for the use of milk paint. Cow's skimmed milk has been used as a base for paint for several thousand years. Egyptians used skim milk, slaked lime, and colors to brighten their buildings. Milk paint was used throughout Europe and followed the early craftsman to the new world.

There were many milk paint formulas which greatly varied the final results. One old basic formula was ½ gallon of skimmed milk, 6 ounces of lime, and 4 ounces of color. This gave a finish that was very coarse and dull in color. The original paint hardened more and more through the years, which makes it almost impossible to remove today.

I highly recommend that you simply order a dry mixture of commercial milk paint that is still made up. The company's name and address is given at the end of this book. Write them for information, prices and paint samples.

The Eighteenth-Century Footstool, the Pennsylvania Dutch Child's Bench, and the Six-Board Blanket Chest, could be painted, not stained, if you would like to try milk paint.

To further achieve an aged effect to either a stained finished or painted finish, a "wash coat" should be applied. The wash coat is simply a mixture of a teaspoon of oil-based black paint mixed with one-half cup of turpentine. This can be stored in a jar with a tight cover for use anytime, and will last for most all projects. Wipe wash over the entire project, let dry, and apply a light coat of tung oil. (Tung oil is similar to varnish, but is applied by hand for a handrub finish. It could also be applied with a cloth. Tung oil allows the wood to "breathe" which, in turn, will cause it to "age" nicely in time.) The wash coat will bring out the "distressing" process, will add years of "dirt" and "dust," and will add seventy-five years to your project. If you want your projects to look new, eliminate both the distressing and wash coat processes.

Eighteenth-Century
Footstool

Footstools come in just about all shapes and sizes. It seems that all woodworkers used their own designs, so you will find very few footstools that are exactly alike. The original of this footstool was made sometime during the eighteenth century. This version is very simple to make and very sturdy. Study the assembly drawing carefully and note the relationship between the five parts. There are two ends (part 1), two side braces (part 2), and one top board (part 3).

MATERIALS

1 1- by 10- by 36-inch #2 pine board
1 ½- by 4- by 30-inch #2 pine board
14 4d finish nails (antique-cut style)
Wood glue
Water putty
Sandpaper, medium and fine
Steel wool, #0000 grade
Stain or milk paint of your choice
Tung oil

CONSTRUCTION

Study the drawing of the ends (part 1). Measure and cut out from the 1- by 10-inch board two ends, each 7½ inches wide by 8½ inches long. Using a try square, make sure that all angles are cut at exactly 90 degrees. Measure the two ½- by 3-inch notches at the top and cut at a 90-degree angle, as shown. Lay out the ½-inch squares, according to the dimensions given, and transfer the leg design to one board. Using a hand coping saw or an electric saber saw, cut out the legs of one side only. Keep close to the marked line, leaving just enough extra wood to sand down to the line. Transfer the shape of the legs you have just cut out to the other end board and cut them out. Try to make both ends exactly the same.

Sand all sides and edges with medium sandpaper. Be very careful not to "round" any edges and to keep all edges sharp at this time. A sanding block is a very helpful tool for this.

From the ½- by 4-inch board, cut out two 3- by 13½-inch boards. Referring to part 2, carefully lay out the ½-inch squares on each end of one of the two boards and transfer the shape as illustrated. Cut out, transfer this shape to the other board, and cut out as above. Sand all sides and edges with medium sandpaper. Again, care must be taken not to "round" any edges.

Referring to part 3, the top board, cut a board 9 inches by 15 inches from the remaining 1- by 10-inch board, taking care to square all corners. Sand with medium sandpaper and "round" corners and top edges slightly as noted.

ASSEMBLY

Add a small amount of glue in the ½- by 3-inch grooves of the two ends (part 1), taking care not to use too much.

Nail the ends and side braces (part 2) together, using four nails per side. Use a try square to check that the legs are "square" (90 degrees) to the side braces and exactly 10½ inches apart. (Refer to the assembly drawing.) Set the footstool upright on its legs and check that all corners are "square" when viewed from the top. It is important to check this before the glue sets. Put a thin film of glue around the entire top of the ends and braces and center the top board (part 3) in place. Carefully nail it in position using three nails per side.

Check your work; wipe any excess glue off with a damp cloth; make sure the stool sets flat on all four legs and does not rock. (Sand along the legs if necessary to level.) Countersink all nails; that is, pound the nail heads about 1/16 inch below the finished surface, using a small size nail set.

FINISHING

Following the directions on the package, mix a small amount of water putty. Fill all countersunk nails and any visible cracks between mating parts. Add only enough to fill the holes and cracks, as all excess putty must be sanded off later. Let dry for ½ hour. Using fine sandpaper and a block sander, sand all putty smooth. "Round" all corners. This will simulate years of wear. Do not try to be exact with the sanding, as some areas wear more than others over the years. Go over the entire stool with #0000 steel wool until the surface feels very smooth. If you decide to "distress" the stool to make it even older, lightly tap here and there with various objects or tools to simulate years of hard use. Sand with steel wool lightly after the "distressing" procedure. Do not be afraid to experiment. The distressing process gives that aged look to your project and is well worth the effort.

Clean the entire work area and wipe the footstool with a clean cloth and a little turpentine. Apply a stain of your choice, such as Ipswich Pine, Early American, or a walnut stain; a colonial paint color could be used if desired. Follow all instructions on the stain or paint can. Let dry for 24 hours and apply a second coat of stain. Let dry for another 24 hours and lightly steel-wool with #0000 grade. Wipe the entire stool. With a damp cloth apply tung oil, one coat at a time. The more coats you apply, the shinier the stool becomes. One or two coats are just about right for an "antique" look.

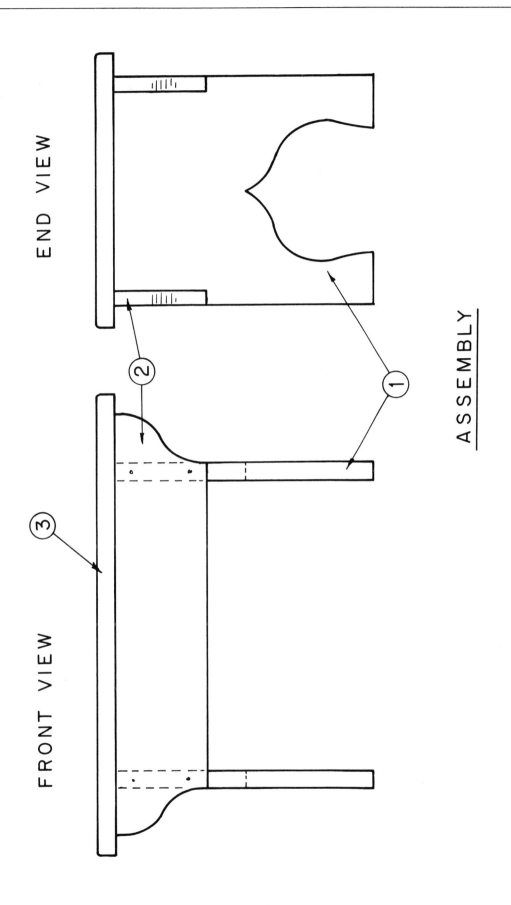

FRONT VIEW

EDGE VIEW

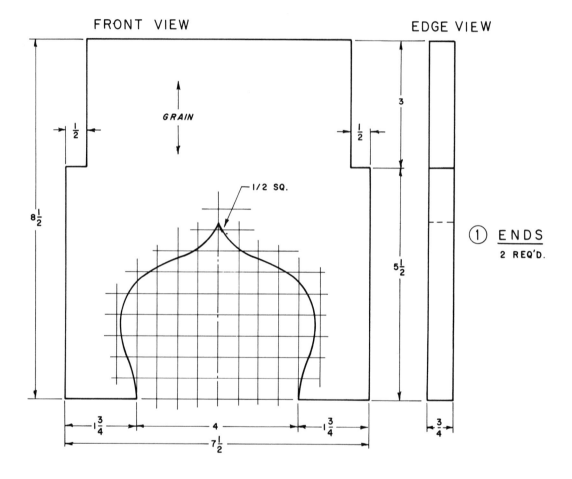

GRAIN

1/2 SQ.

① ENDS
2 REQ'D.

FRONT VIEW

EDGE VIEW

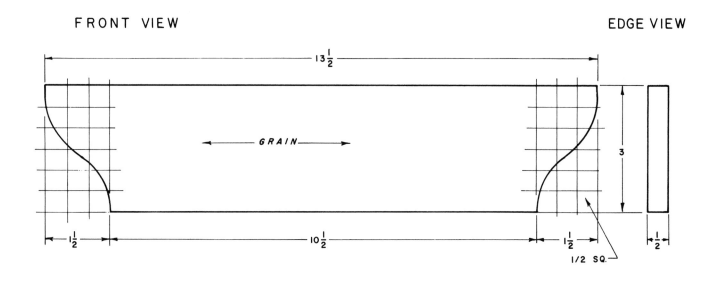

$13\frac{1}{2}$

GRAIN

3

$1\frac{1}{2}$

$10\frac{1}{2}$

$1\frac{1}{2}$

$\frac{1}{2}$

1/2 SQ.

② SIDE BRACES
2 REQ'D.

TOP VIEW

ROUND CORNERS AS SHOWN — EDGE VIEW

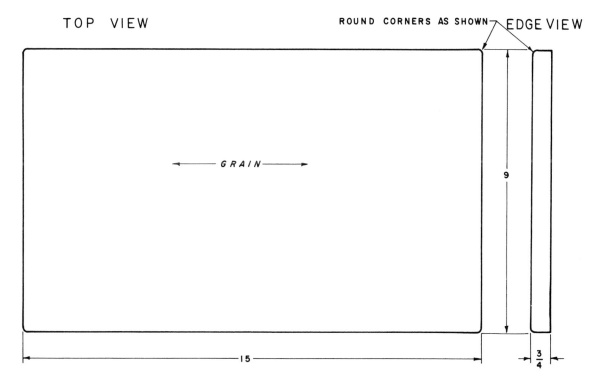

GRAIN

9

15

$\frac{3}{4}$

③ TOP BOARD

Shaker Candleholder

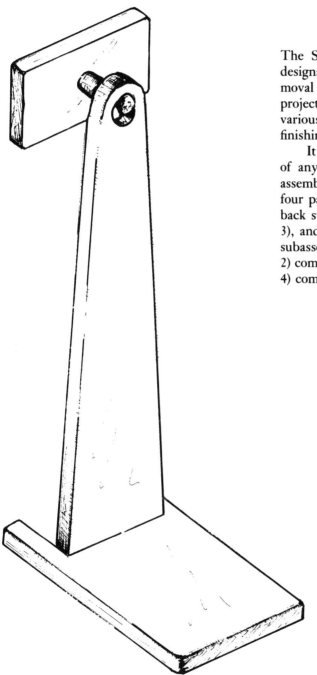

The Shakers were noted for their simple, functional designs. This candleholder was designed for easy removal from the wall. Because it is simple, this is a good project to start with. It will give you practice in using various tools and will enable you to practice the art of finishing a wood surface.

It is important that you understand the construction of any project before beginning. Carefully study the assembly drawing and note the relationship between the four parts. There is one of each of the following parts: back support (part 1), base (part 2), wall support (part 3), and peg (part 4). Notice that there are actually two subassemblies: the back support (part 1) and base (part 2) comprise one, the wall support (part 3) and peg (part 4) comprise the other.

MATERIALS

1 1- by 6-inch by 3-foot #2 pine board
1 ¾-inch by 3-inch dowel
2 4d finish nails (antique-cut style)
Wood glue
Water putty
Sandpaper, medium and fine
Steel wool, #0000 grade
Stain of your choice
Tung oil

CONSTRUCTION

Study the drawing of the back support (part 1). Measure, "square," and cut 18 inches from the 36-inch board. Cut the 6-inch side, 4½ inches wide, so you have a piece of wood 4½ inches by 18 inches. Measure and locate the 1-inch-diameter hole (2⅛ inches from each side), using a compass. Scribe the 1-inch radius from the hole center before drilling the hole. From the other end, measure up 1 inch on each side. From this point, draw a straight line so it just passes by the 1-inch radius at the other end. Carefully cut out, as shown, with a hand coping saw or an electric saber saw. Stay just outside the line as you cut, leaving enough extra wood to sand down to the line.

Sand all sides and edges with medium sandpaper. Try not to "round" the edges at this time.

Refer to the base drawing (part 2). From the remaining wood, measure, "square," and cut off 9 inches. Carefully, using the "square," locate the 2½- by 4¼-inch-size cutout (1¹¹⁄₁₆ inch in from the sides). Sand all sides and edges with medium sandpaper. Round all edges, as shown (approximately ⅛-inch radius).

ASSEMBLY

Check that part 1 fits tightly with part 2. Use a small amount of glue to glue part 1 and part 2 together, taking care that there is exactly a 90-degree angle between the two parts. Nail the parts together and wipe off all excess glue with a damp cloth. If necessary, mix up a small amount of water putty and add to make a tight joint. Sand all putty off after it dries.

The wall support (part 3) is very simple to make. Measure, "square," and cut a piece of wood 3 by 6 inches. Carefully locate the ⅜-inch-diameter hole (½ inches from bottom edge and 3 inches in from sides, as shown). Drill the ⅜-inch-diameter hole and carefully sand. Notice the edges that are rounded; notice the edges that face the wall are not rounded.

Refer to the pin (part 4). This part will give you an opportunity to try your hand at carving with a sharp jackknife or a comparable tool. Carve the pin as close as possible to the way it is shown in the illustration. The only critical part would be the ⅜-inch-diameter portion; be sure to keep a sharp transition between it and the 1¹⁄₁₆-inch diameter. This is important in order for the pin to fit flush and tight against the wall support (part 3). Using a small amount of glue, glue the pin to the wall support. Wipe any excess glue with a damp cloth.

If you plan to attach the wall support subassembly to the wall with screws, it is best to drill the holes for the screws at this time. (Drilling 2 inches each side of the ⅜-inch-diameter hole is recommended.)

FINISHING

Follow the finishing procedure as outlined for the Eighteenth-Century Footstool.

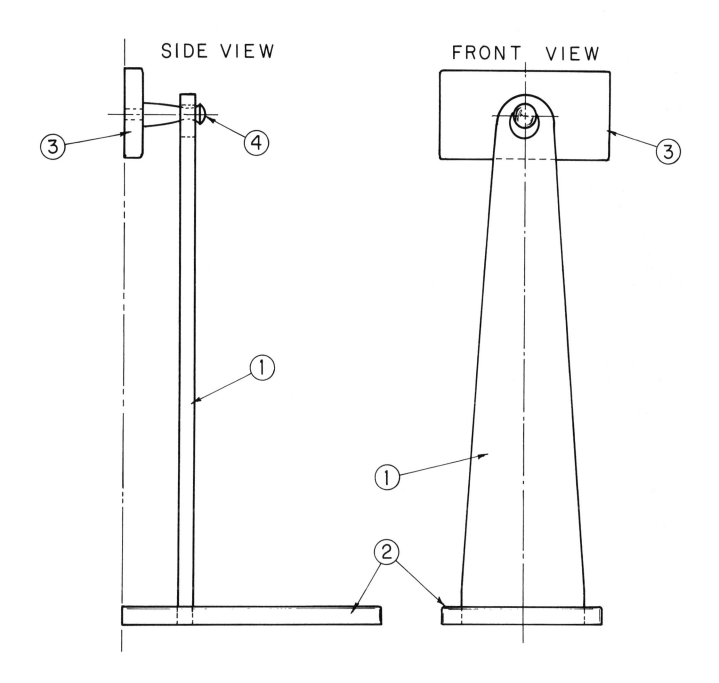

SIDE VIEW

FRONT VIEW

ASSEMBLY

FRONT VIEW

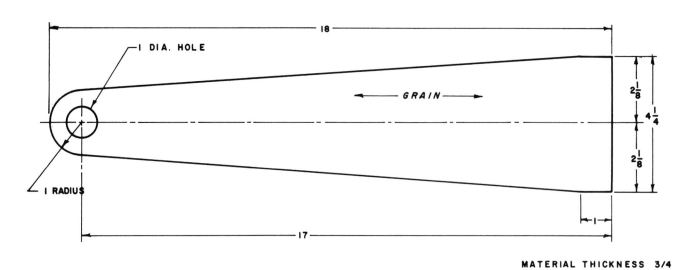

MATERIAL THICKNESS 3/4

① <u>BACK SUPPORT</u>
I REQ'D.

FRONT VIEW   EDGE VIEW

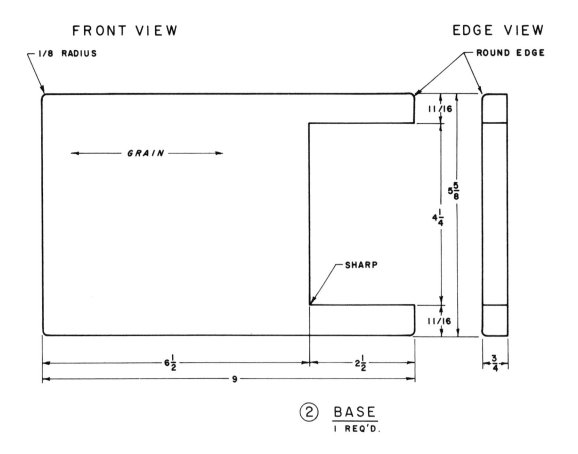

② <u>BASE</u>
I REQ'D.

FRONT VIEW   EDGE VIEW

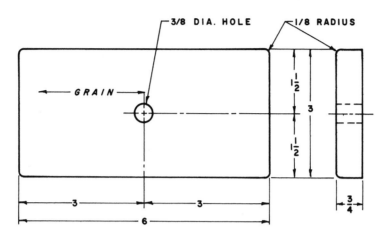

③ WALL SUPPORT
I REQ'D.

SIDE VIEW   END VIEW

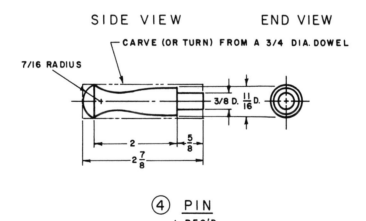

④ PIN
I REQ'D.

Three-Rail Towel Rack

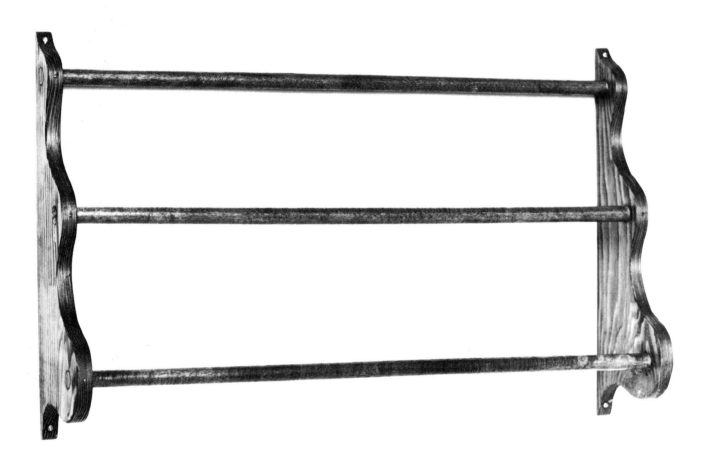

This towel rack was found in northern Vermont in a barn "milk house." It blends into an antique setting just beautifully. The rack can be shortened or lengthened to fit any area perfectly, and a two-rail towel rack can be made by omitting the bottom rail and slightly modifying the two sides.

Study the assembly drawing and notice how the parts are nailed together. These nails will show, so I recommend that you use antique-style nails, if possible.

MATERIALS

1 1- by 6-inch by 3-foot #2 pine board
3 ¾- by 36-inch dowels
6 old-fashioned cut nails, fine-cut headless brads, ¼ inches long
Wood glue
Water putty
Sandpaper, medium and fine
Steel wool, #0000 grade
Stain of your choice
Tung oil

CONSTRUCTION

The side (part 1) shape must be transferred to the 1- by 6-inch piece of wood.

Using a scale and a square, carefully draw the 1-inch "squares." Be sure to add the grid, or squares, very lightly, as this will have to be completely sanded off later.

Position the three ¾-inch-diameter hole centers first. Simply count the squares according to the plan. (Example: the bottom hole is located three squares up and 4 ¾ inch squares over.) Carefully locate the other two holes. Starting from either end, locate the outline of the side from square to square. Double-check your progress, especially near the ¾-inch-diameter hole locations.

Before cutting the side out, drill the three ¾-inch-diameter holes. Care must be taken in drilling the holes. Drill from one side until the drill tip just starts through the back surface, and stop drilling. Turn the board over and complete the drilling process. This is an important "trick" and is used so the back side will not split as the drill pushes through. Remember this "trick," as it should be used any time a hole is drilled through any part.

Use a hand jigsaw or an electric saber saw to cut one side, taking care to cut close to the lines so you can sand down to them later.

Using the first side as a template, trace the first side on the remaining wood. It is important that the three small ¹⁄₁₆-inch-diameter holes be drilled before proceeding. Locate the center of the edge surface and drill toward the center of the ¾-inch-diameter holes. Note that there are two ⅛-inch-diameter holes drilled 90 degrees to the back surface and located ½ inch from the top and bottom of the part. Extreme care must be taken, as the wood is very weak at these points.

Using a ¼-inch-diameter drill as a "counterbore," start the ¼-inch-diameter drill into the ⅛-inch-diameter drilled hole and just break the surface. This "counterbored" hole is to provide a flat surface for the four screws used later to attach the shelf to the wall.

Sand all sides and edges with medium sandpaper. Do not "round" the back edges; that is, the edge that goes against the wall. Do not try to be exact with sanding of the edges. Antique racks are surely worn more in some areas than in other areas.

ASSEMBLY

Cut the three ¾-inch-diameter dowels and lightly sand the cut ends. Using a small amount of glue, assemble the three dowels into the two sides. Be sure to support the sides on a smooth, flat, surface as you proceed to check that both sides are in line. Wipe all excess glue off and nail through the six small ¹⁄₁₆-inch-diameter holes into the dowels. If the dowels are too hard, drill the holes before nailing so you do not split the wood.

Do not try to hide the six nails; antique-cut nails should show. Fill any other cracks with water putty and sand away all excess putty.

FINISHING

Follow the finishing procedure outlined for the Eighteenth-Century Footstool

SIDE VIEW   FRONT VIEW

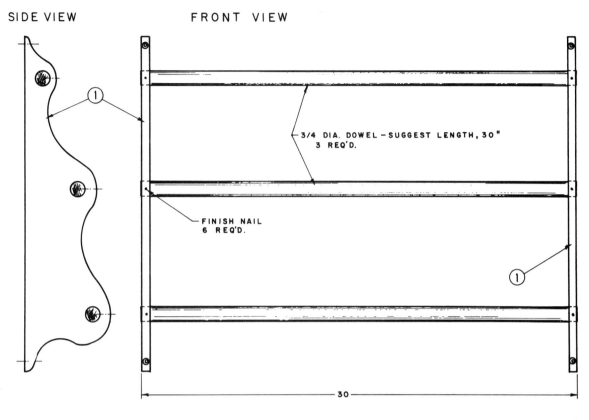

3/4 DIA. DOWEL – SUGGEST LENGTH, 30"
3 REQ'D.

FINISH NAIL
6 REQ'D.

30

ASSEMBLY

1/8 DIA. HOLE – 1/4 DIA. COUNTERBORE
(DEEP ENOUGH TO PROVIDE A FLAT SURFACE)
2 REQ'D.

1/16 DIA. HOLE, 3 REQ'D.

TOP VIEW

3/4

18

FRONT VIEW

3/4 DIA. HOLE
3 REQ'D.

1" SQ.

6

G R A I N

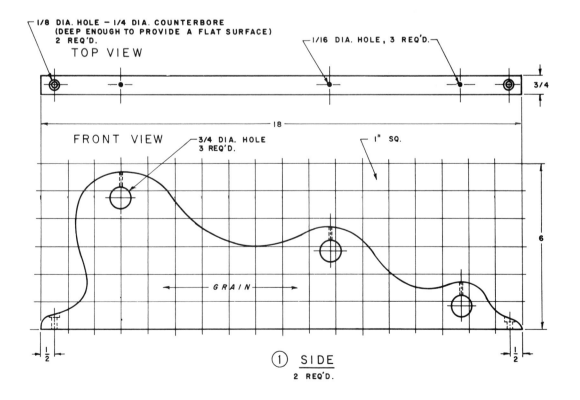

½   ½

① SIDE
2 REQ'D.

Silverware Tray

This authentic silverware tray was very popular around the year 1820. A visit to any flea market will uncover two or three of these trays for thirty to forty dollars each. Why they faded from popularity is a mystery because they are handy to have and use. It is fairly easy to make each part, but assembly requires about five hands!

Study the assembly drawing. Notice that the inside of parts 1 and 2 are sanded after assembly. Study the five parts. Be sure you fully understand each part before beginning.

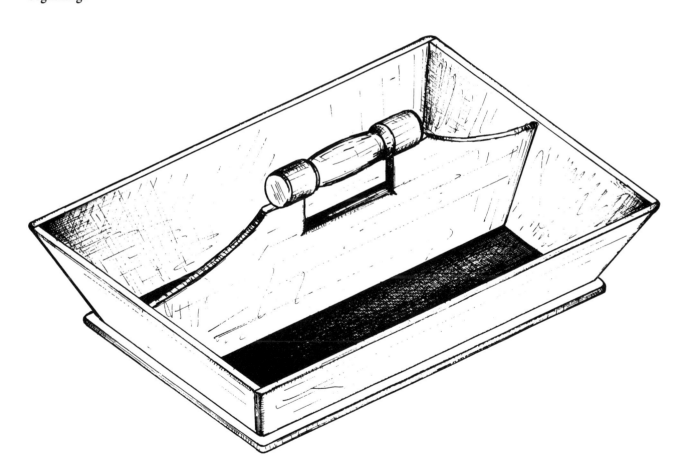

MATERIALS

1 ¼- by 8-inch by 4-foot #2 pine board
1 ¹¹⁄₁₆-inch-diameter dowel
22 old-fashioned cut nails, fine-cut headless brads, 1¼ inches long
Wood glue
Water putty
Sandpaper, medium and fine
Steel wool, #0000 grade
Stain of your choice
Tung oil

CONSTRUCTION

The ¼-inch thick wood could be a problem to find. A 1- by 8-inch by 4-foot board could be split in two, if you have a table saw. If not, I suggest a visit to the local high school industrial arts class. Most instructors would be happy to run your board through their planer (provided they have one). You may want to bring along two or three short boards to be planed at the same time, as many projects use these thinner boards.

Carefully measure and plan where the parts will be located.

For part 1, measure the sides, using the dimensions on the detail plan. Care must be taken in making the bottom exactly a 25-degree angle. If you have a table saw, simply set and cut at 25 degrees. If you do not have a table saw, use a hand plane to obtain the 25 degrees.

For part 2, measure the end, using the dimensions on the detail plan. Study the detail drawing carefully. Notice that the bottom is tapered 25 degrees (see end view) and the two sides 10 degrees (see top view).

For part 3, carefully and lightly locate the ½-inch-square grid and transfer the shape to the wood. If you plan to make more than one tray, it is a good idea to make a cardboard pattern. Important: Cut the overall length to 12³⁄₁₆ inches or so. Trim it down to 12⅛ inches at time of assembly to ensure a good, tight fit.

For part 4, cut a ¹¹⁄₁₆-inch dowel approximately 8 inches long and, using a sharp knife, carve the approximate shape as shown. Remember that most silverware trays were homemade and most were handmade. Carving will give you that authentic, crude appearance. The extra length is to give you something to hold while carving. Trim to 4 inches long after sanding smooth. Be sure to add the two flat surfaces (see end view).

To obtain the ³⁄₁₆ inch thickness for part 5, you can either sand or plane to the desired thickness. Round the edges with a plane as shown.

ASSEMBLY

Be sure that corners of the sides (part 1) and the ends (part 2) fit fairly tight without any gaps. Glue the two sides and the two ends together. Use large rubber bands to hold until the glue sets. After glue has set, carefully drill two small holes at each corner of the sides (part 1) for the antique-cut nails. Insert nails, but do not countersink. Allow the nails to show.

Sand the bottom of parts 1 and parts 2 so that there is a smooth, flat surface at the bottom. "Round" the top, inside and outside, as shown on the assembly drawing. Put a thin film of glue around the bottom surfaces of parts 1 and 2 and center bottom (part 5). Allow the glue to set. Carefully drill eight holes through part 5 from the bottom, at an angle, in line with parts 1 and 2 (approximately 25 degrees). Insert nails (again, do not countersink), allowing nails to show. Attach handle (part 4) to divider (part 3), using glue and two nails. (Drill dowel first.)

The center divider (part 3) was made a bit oversize. Check for fit by sliding into place. Trim ends until divider fits perfectly in place and touches the sides and bottom snugly. Remove and add a thin film of glue to the sides and bottom. Allow glue to set and nail through from each end with two nails per end. It should not be necessary to drill holes first. This is a good time to practice "distressing." These silverware trays saw a lot of use through the years. Rarely will you find one in perfect condition.

Fill all corners with wood putty, if necessary, and sand smooth.

FINISHING

Follow the finishing procedure as outlined for the Eighteenth-Century Footstool.

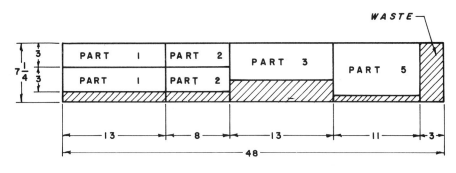

SUGGESTED CUTS

FRONT VIEW

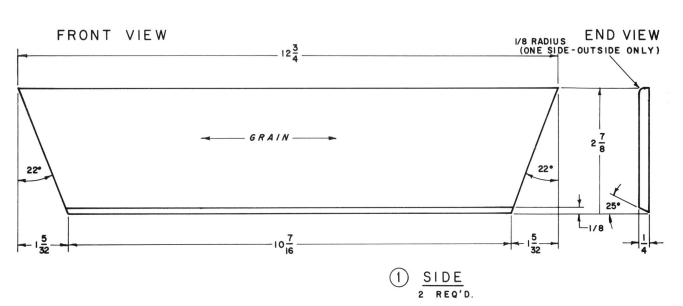

ASSEMBLY

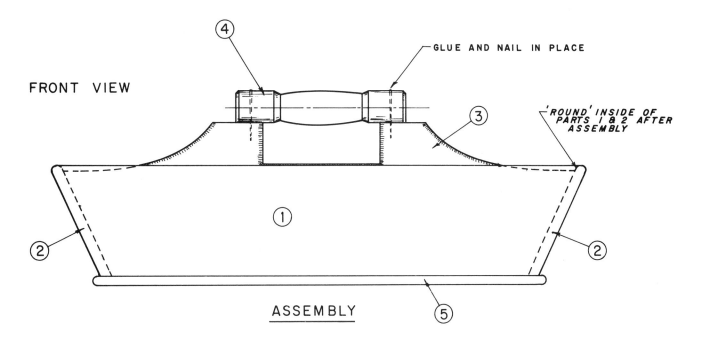

FRONT VIEW

END VIEW

① SIDE
2 REQ'D.

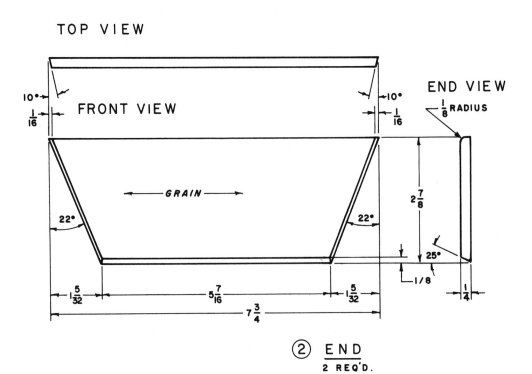

TOP VIEW

FRONT VIEW

END VIEW

② <u>END</u>
2 REQ'D.

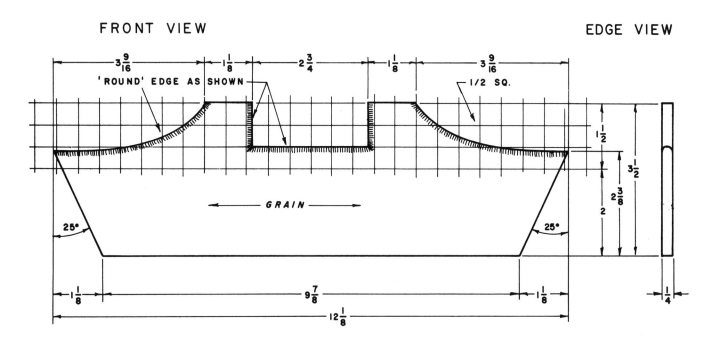

FRONT VIEW

EDGE VIEW

③ <u>CENTER DIVIDER</u>
1 REQ'D.

FRONT VIEW   END VIEW

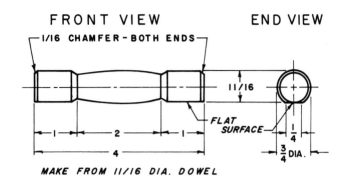

1/16 CHAMFER-BOTH ENDS

11/16

FLAT SURFACE

1   2   1

4

$\frac{1}{4}$

$\frac{3}{4}$ DIA.

MAKE FROM 11/16 DIA. DOWEL

④ HANDLE

1 REQ'D.

FRONT VIEW   EDGE VIEW

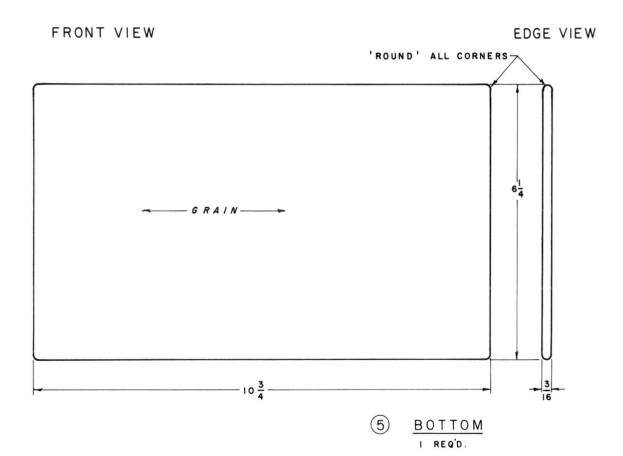

'ROUND' ALL CORNERS

← GRAIN →

$6\frac{1}{4}$

$10\frac{3}{4}$

$\frac{3}{16}$

⑤ BOTTOM

1 REQ'D.

"Lollipop" Candle Box

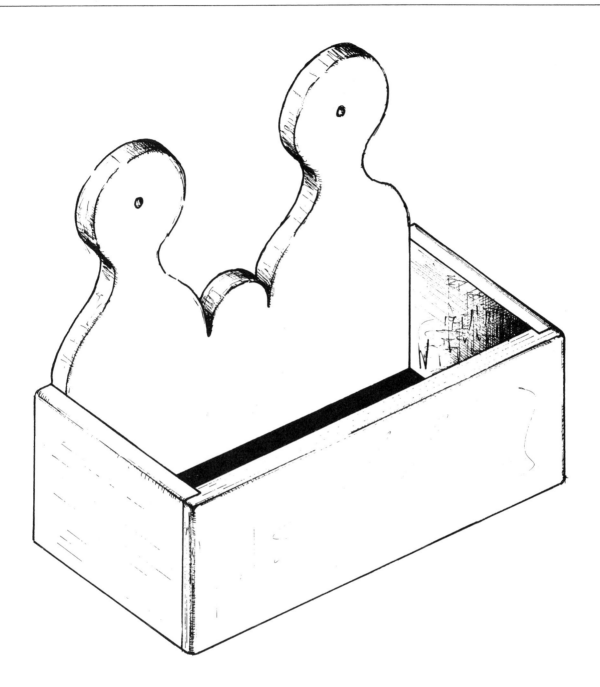

A functional addition to any wall is the candle box. In the eighteenth century candle boxes were made in many styles and designs. The double "lollipop," relatively simple to construct and finish, is a bit different and has a unique design. It makes a beautiful plant holder.

Take a few minutes and study the assembly drawing. Be sure you understand how the candle box is put together before starting. The project has four different parts and, except for the back board (part 1), all are very simple to make.

Note: This project uses ½-inch-thick material.

MATERIAL
1½- by 12-inch by 2-foot #2 pine board
16 old-fashioned cut nails, fine-cut headless brads, 1¼ inches long
Wood glue
Wood putty
Sandpaper, medium and fine
Steel wool, #0000 grade
Stain of your choice
Tung oil

CONSTRUCTION
The hardest part to make is the back board (part 1). Start by measuring and squaring a board 11 by 11 inches. Care should be taken in the grain direction. (Note the "direction of grain" arrow.)

Carefully, measure off the ½-inch grid lightly (or make a cardboard pattern, if you plan to make more than one).

Using a compass, swing the two 1½-inch radii from the correct swing points (three squares down, five squares in from the sides). Swing the 1-inch radius from the center using a compass. After these three compass swings have been made, draw in the rest of the "lollipops." Take care that both sides match perfectly. Drill the two ¼-inch-diameter holes and sand with medium paper. Do not "round" any surfaces at this time.

From the remaining wood, choose an interesting grain or knot feature and lay out the front (part 3). Notice the two ¼- by ½-inch notches at either end (top view). If you have a table saw, the notches can be cut very easily, but a hand saw does the job just as well. Be sure the notch has sharp inside corners. Sand all surfaces.

Cut the two ends (part 2) absolutely "square." Sand all sides and edges.

Part 4 bottom should be cut "square" also, but it is a good idea to make it a bit oversize to start with. Sand, plane, or cut it to fit at assembly.

ASSEMBLY
Check to see that all parts fit snugly together. Sand or file any parts that do not.

Notice that the ends (part 2) go on the outside of the rear (part 1). The front (part 3) fits into the ends (part 2). Glue and nail parts 1, 2, and 3 together, using two nails at each joint. Do not try to hide these nails. Let them show for that authentic antique look. Be sure these three parts are square before glue sets.

The bottom is now ready to be installed. There should be a tight fit against the front (part 3) and the rack board (part 1). However, allow a slight space between the bottom and the end (part 2) for expansion of the bottom. After checking for fit, apply glue to the front and back edges of bottom only. Slide up into place and add two nails in from the ends only. The glue will hold the front and rear in place.

Fill all seams with wood putty and completely sand all excess glue and putty off. With thought as to where the edges on an old piece would have worn throughout the years, use a rasp to round the front edges of the back board to suit. "Distress" all other surfaces and sand using the fine paper, followed by a good rubdown with #0000 steel wool.

FINISHING
Follow the finishing procedures as outlined for the Eighteenth-Century Footstool.

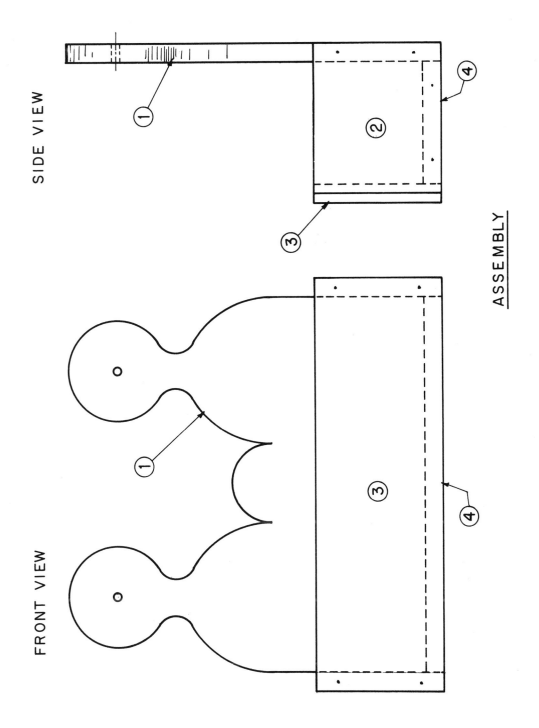

SIDE VIEW

FRONT VIEW

ASSEMBLY

FRONT VIEW   EDGE VIEW

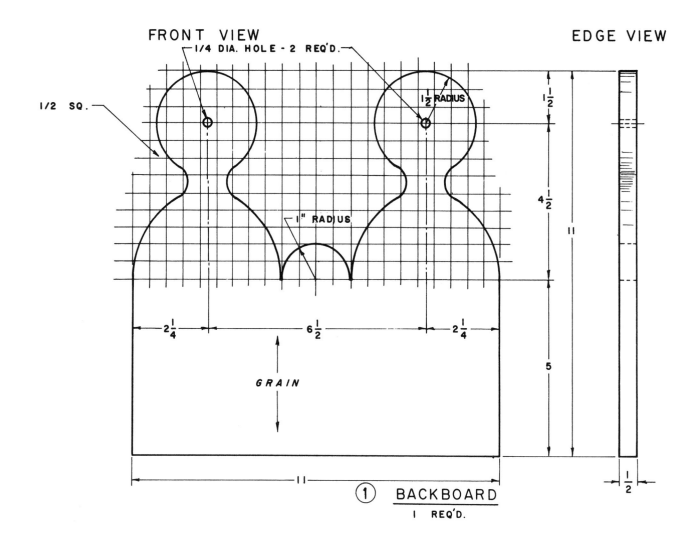

1/4 DIA. HOLE - 2 REQ'D.

1/2 SQ.

1½ RADIUS

1" RADIUS

1½

4½

11

2¼   6½   2¼

5

GRAIN

11

½

① <u>BACKBOARD</u>
1 REQ'D.

FRONT VIEW   EDGE VIEW

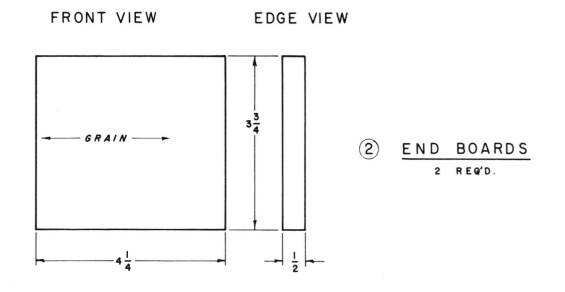

GRAIN

3¾

② <u>END BOARDS</u>
2 REQ'D.

4¼

½

TOP VIEW

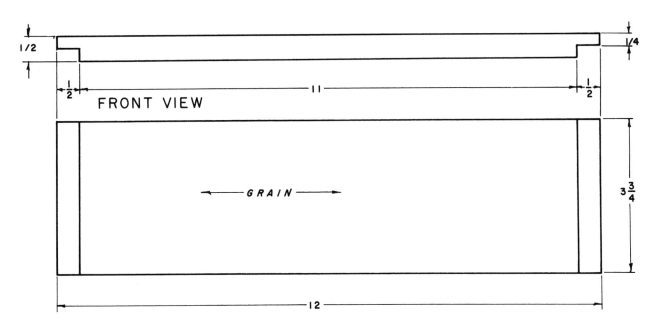

FRONT VIEW

1/2

1/4

½

11

½

GRAIN

3¾

12

③ FRONT BOARD
1 REQ'D.

FRONT VIEW

EDGE VIEW

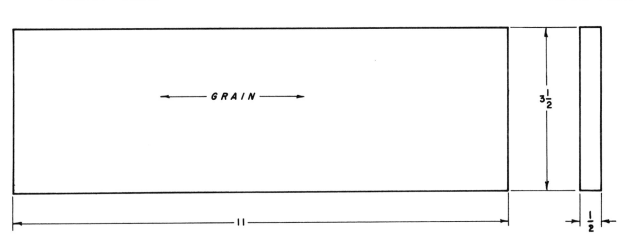

GRAIN

3½

11

½

④ BOTTOM BOARD
1 REQ'D.

Shaker Drying Rack

With the return of the wood stove, it follows logically that drying racks will be in demand. The drying rack adds a special touch to the area around your wood stove. Even better, this project will probably be one of your most useful projects, especially if you have small children running in and out all winter. Wet mittens and socks drying by the stove add an air of nostalgia to your room.

There are many styles of drying racks. Most have fancy turnings, but this particular rack was one of the first styles used and is considered a primitive piece of furniture. This project has been taken directly from an original drying rack and is the exact same size.

The only problem that you may encounter in making this rack will be locating the odd sizes of wood. For 100% authenticity, you should try to make the dryer exactly as dimensioned. There are actually only three different parts in this entire project, so it can be made in little time at all. As with most projects, finishing should take longer than the actual making and assembly time.

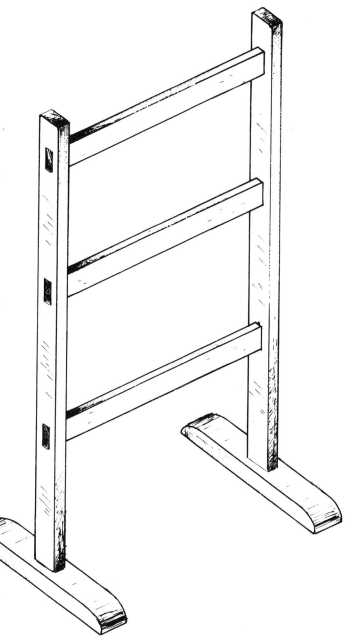

MATERIALS

1 2- by 6- by 14-inch #2 pine board
1 ⁵⁄₄- by 3-inch by 6-foot #2 pine board
1 1- by 2-inch by 6-foot #2 pine board
12 old-fashioned cut nails, fine-cut headless brads, 1¼ inch long
Wood glue
Wood putty
Sandpaper, medium and fine
Steel wool, #0000 grade
Stain of your choice
Tung oil

Note: The ⁵⁄₄-inch thickness is used for shelves and should be in stock at most lumberyards. If not available, inquire at the local Industrial Arts Department at a nearby high school. A standard 2 × 4 (1½ by 3½) could be used, although it is usually spruce, not pine. Two ¾-inch-thick boards could be glued together as a last resort.

CONSTRUCTION

From the 2- by 6-inch piece cut out the two feet (part 1), each 1½ inches high by 2¼ inches wide by 13 inches long. Lay out the "rounded" ends using the ¼-inch-square grid, but anything close to this shape will be all right.

The "square" hole in each foot must be the exact size of the side boards (part 2). Be sure these holes are centered. Sand smoothly with the medium sandpaper. A square hole is accomplished by drilling a series of ¹³⁄₁₆-inch-diameter holes inside the square. Using a sharp chisel, carefully chisel in from both sides. Square-up with a rasp and try to stay just inside of the square. Sand the hole to the exact size at assembly with the two side boards (part 2). Strive for a good, tight fit. This will be true with the three holes in the two side boards also.

Cut the two side boards (part 2) to size. Carefully locate and mark the three square holes in the side of the two boards. They should match each other exactly.

Using the same procedure as outlined for part 1, chisel, rasp, and sand the six holes. Again, try to keep the holes just a little too small. Fit them at assembly.

Do not forget to cut the two ¼-inch- by 45-degree-angle chamfers at the top end of the side boards, as illustrated.

Measure, square, and cut the three bars (part 3). Sand all sides with medium paper.

ASSEMBLY

The drying rack is now ready for assembly. Lightly sand the inside of the cut-out squared holes so that each mating part fits snugly. After you have checked all fits, lightly glue the two side boards (part 2) and the three bars together. Work on a smooth, flat surface so there is no warpage of these five parts. Use one nail at each side of each joint to help the glue hold the rack together. Let these five parts dry thoroughly in a flat position.

After the glue has set, add the two feet. Check to see that the side boards (part 2) are set at exactly 90 degrees to the feet (part 1).

Add water putty to all joints and sand smooth. Because drying racks are so old, don't be afraid to distress all surfaces before the final sanding.

FINISHING

Follow the finishing procedure as outlined for the Eighteenth-Century Footstool.

To achieve that "aged" look add burnt umber oil paint (directly from an artist's collection of paint tubes). Starting from each joint, add color with your finger, extending about 1 to 2 inches from each joint and fanning out completely. Practice until you get the effect you want. Don't worry, if you don't like the result. It can be wiped off before it dries! When you are satisfied, let the oil paint dry thoroughly before adding the tung oil. This procedure can be used to highlight the edges, too.

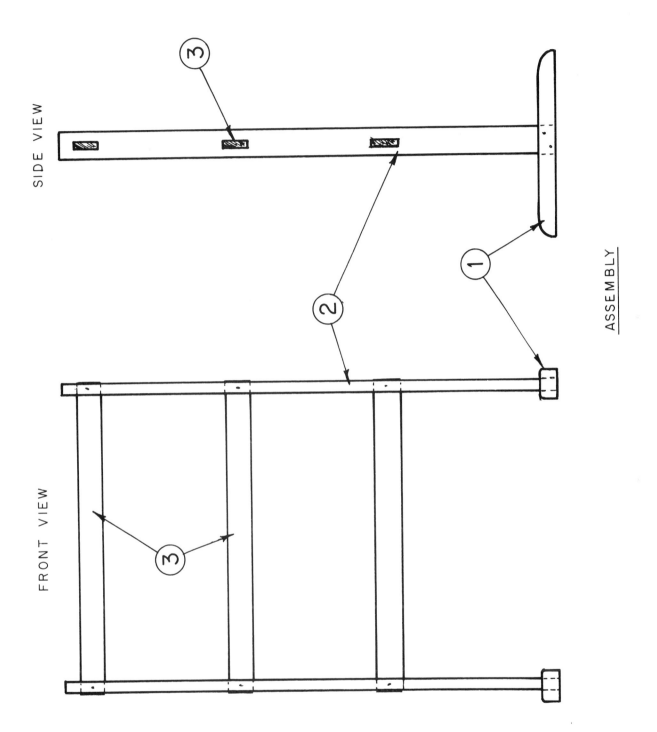

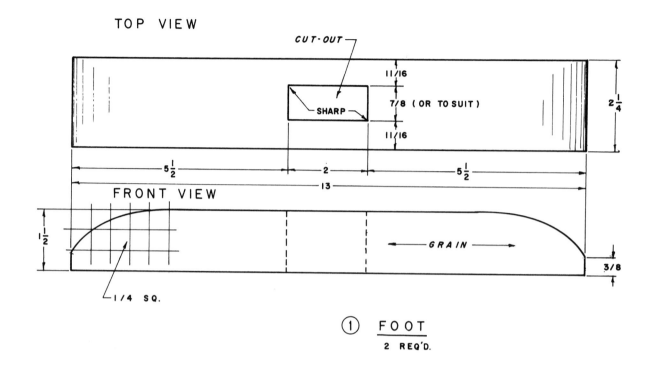

TOP VIEW

CUT-OUT

SHARP

11/16

7/8 (OR TO SUIT)

11/16

2 1/4

FRONT VIEW

1 1/2

5 1/2

2

5 1/2

13

GRAIN

3/8

1/4 SQ.

① FOOT
2 REQ'D.

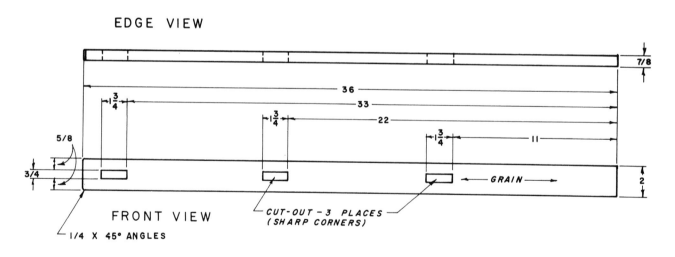

EDGE VIEW

7/8

36

33

1 3/4

22

1 3/4

11

1 3/4

5/8

3/4

GRAIN

2

FRONT VIEW

CUT-OUT - 3 PLACES
(SHARP CORNERS)

1/4 X 45° ANGLES

② SIDE BOARDS
2 REQ'D.

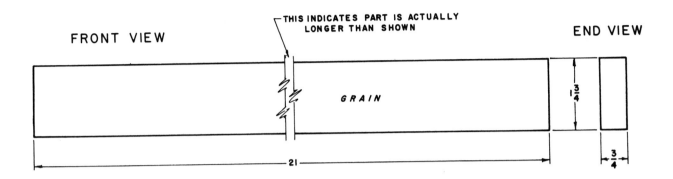

FRONT VIEW

THIS INDICATES PART IS ACTUALLY
LONGER THAN SHOWN

GRAIN

END VIEW

$1\frac{3}{4}$

21

$\frac{3}{4}$

③ BARS
3 REQ'D.

Chippendale Mirror Frame

A very expensive piece of Americana is the Chippendale mirror. These were made originally in sizes from 10 inches wide and 18 inches high, up to 30 inches wide and 60 inches high. The size of this particular project is approximately 16½ by 25 inches. This style was popular from around 1760 to 1810. Many original Chippendale mirrors included a gilded bird at the top as a final flourish. They often had beveled edges, heavy glass, and were up to ⅛ inch thick.

Parts 4 and 5, the frame, have been simplified. The original frames were quite complicated and intricate, thus making construction more difficult. So that it would be both easier to make and stronger than the original, construction of this project has been simplified. Chippendale mirrors were usually made of mahogany, so this might be a good time for you to try a wood other than pine. If you use mahogany, the grain of the wood must be filled before finishing. Fill grain with paste wood filler, following instructions that are provided with product.

MATERIALS

1 ⅜- by 10- by 66-inch wood
1 11- by 14-inch mirror (approximate)
2 #8 flat-head brass screws, ⅝ inch long
Wood glue
Water putty
Sandpaper, medium and fine
Steel wool, #0000 grade
Stain of your choice
Tung oil

Note: The exact size of the mirror glass should be determined later. Purchase glass after assembly.

CONSTRUCTION

Notice the ⅜-inch thickness of wood. This could be a problem unless you can get ⅜-inch-thick wood or have ½-inch wood planed down to ⅜-inch size. Rip an ¹¹⁄₁₆-inch strip off the entire length of the 5- to 6-foot board before starting. (This will be parts 4 and 5.)

Parts 1, 2, and 3 will give you good practice in using a coping saw or saber saw. Roughly cut out the four parts: (one of part 1, two of part 2, and one of part 3). Lightly add the ½-inch grid and transfer the shape from the book to the wood. If you stray from the pattern a little, do not worry as long as both sides match. The only important dimensions on part 1 are the 7½ inches and the two 2¾ inches. The 45-degree-angle cut must be exact. On part 2 the dimensions that must be done with care are the 10½ inches, 4 inches, and 3¾ inches. This 45-degree-angle cut must be exact, also. Because there are two parts, they must be exactly the same. Care must be taken when cutting around the top and bottom scroll, as these are very weak and could break.

Taking care not to "round" any edges, sand all mating surfaces. Fit parts 1, 2, and 3 together on a flat surface. It is hard to make the four parts so that they fit exactly, but the fit should be as tight as possible. These joints will not show, but a tight fit is always preferable to loose joints. If this fit is as close as you can get it, glue the four parts together, using a flat surface as a "base," while the glue is setting. (A piece of plywood is good for this.)

After the glue has dried, add water putty to all joints (both sides). After all putty has hardened, sand both front and back surfaces smooth. Be sure to remove all glue and water putty. After assembly, you will sand all edges with fine sandpaper, taking care not to "round" the edges at this time. Be sure to have a smooth surface at the edges, where the mating parts meet. Study both sides and choose which would make the best front. After

determining the front, carefully "round" all edges (front surface only). Take your time and be careful not to break any of the fine scroll work off.

Parts 4 and 5 are cut from the 1¹⁄₁₆-inch board. The ⅛- by ⁵⁄₁₆-inch groove should be cut at this time. If you have only hand tools, this can be achieved with a plane. It is a long process, however. A table saw will rip this groove out, without any problem. "Round" the top surface with the plane to the approximate shape and sand smooth. Carefully cut the four boards at the 45-degree angle. (Be sure the cuts are into or toward the groove.) Without picture frame cutting equipment, 45-degree cuts are rather difficult, at least the first time, to cut exact. Come as close as possible, and sand to fit, if necessary.

ASSEMBLY

Center the frame, two of part 4 and two of part 5, on the base. Be sure to line up the 45-degree-angle cuts of the frame with the 45-degree-angle cuts of parts 1, 2, and 3. (See assembly drawing.) Mark frame in place; glue the bottom (part 5) and two sides (part 4) in place. Check the top space by using the top piece, but do not glue. After the glue hardens, mark where the top molding is to be located. Remove top molding approximately in the center of where it is to be placed. Drill two ⅛-inch-diameter holes through the base approximately 2 inches in from the top end of the two side frames. Countersink the two holes from the back of the base. Attach the top frame with the two flat-head screws (from the back). Water putty all joints of the frame. Allow to dry and sand completely.

FINISHING

Completely finish all surfaces with the #0000 steel wool. Add stain, making sure not to forget the groove area upon which the mirror will rest. Otherwise bare wood will reflect in the mirror. Add tung oil to suit and completely "finish" the project. Stain the back surface, but do not add tung oil.

After everything is thoroughly dry, remove the two brass screws and the top molding. Measure the inside (left, right, top, bottom) of the groove. Cut a piece of cardboard this size. Slide it down into place from the top and replace the top molding. (The size will be close to 11 by 14 inches.) Using the cardboard as a pattern, have a piece of mirror cut to size from a local hardware store. Add cardboard to the back of the mirror for a spacer, if needed. Hang the mirror as you would hang any mirror or picture frame.

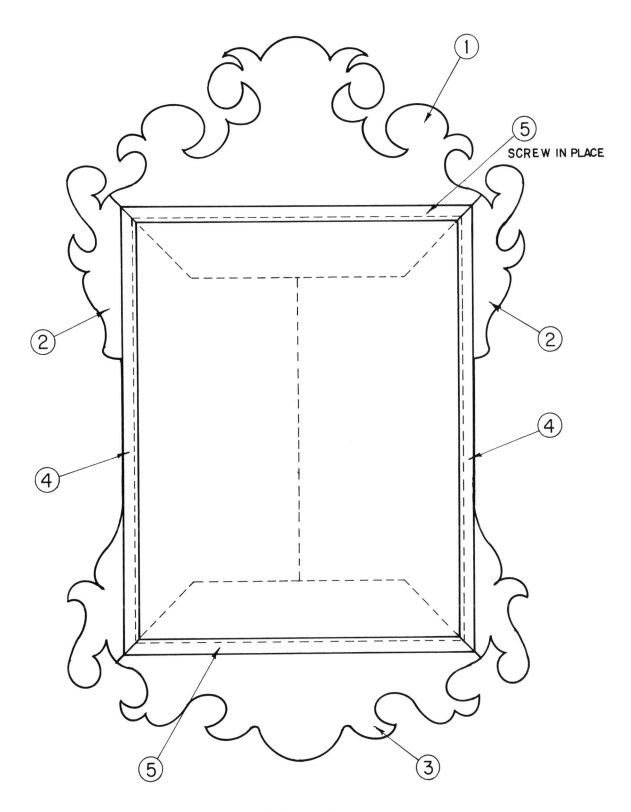

SCREW IN PLACE

ASSEMBLY

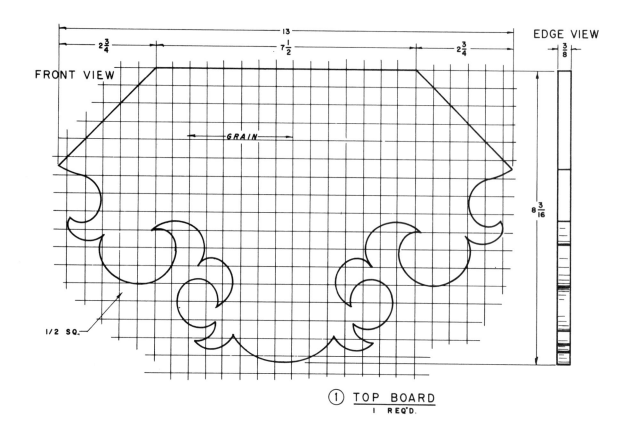

① TOP BOARD
1 REQ'D.

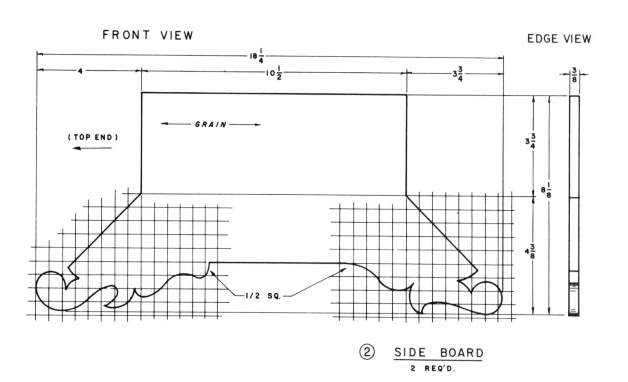

② SIDE BOARD
2 REQ'D.

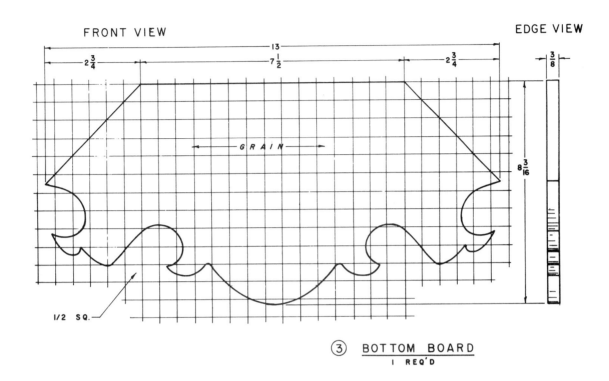

FRONT VIEW

EDGE VIEW

GRAIN

13

2¾ 7½ 2¾

8³⁄₁₆

³⁄₈

1/2 SQ.

③ BOTTOM BOARD
1 REQ'D

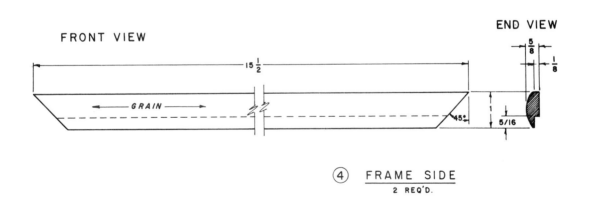

FRONT VIEW

END VIEW

GRAIN

15½

45°

5⁄8

1⁄8

1

5/16

④ FRAME SIDE
2 REQ'D.

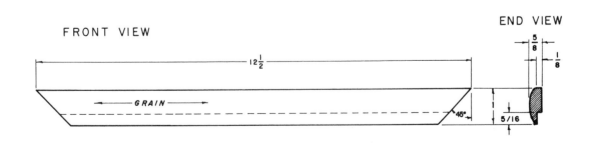

FRONT VIEW

END VIEW

GRAIN

12½

45°

5⁄8

1⁄8

5/16

⑤ FRAME TOP/BOTTOM
2 REQ'D.

Three-Shelf Wall Rack

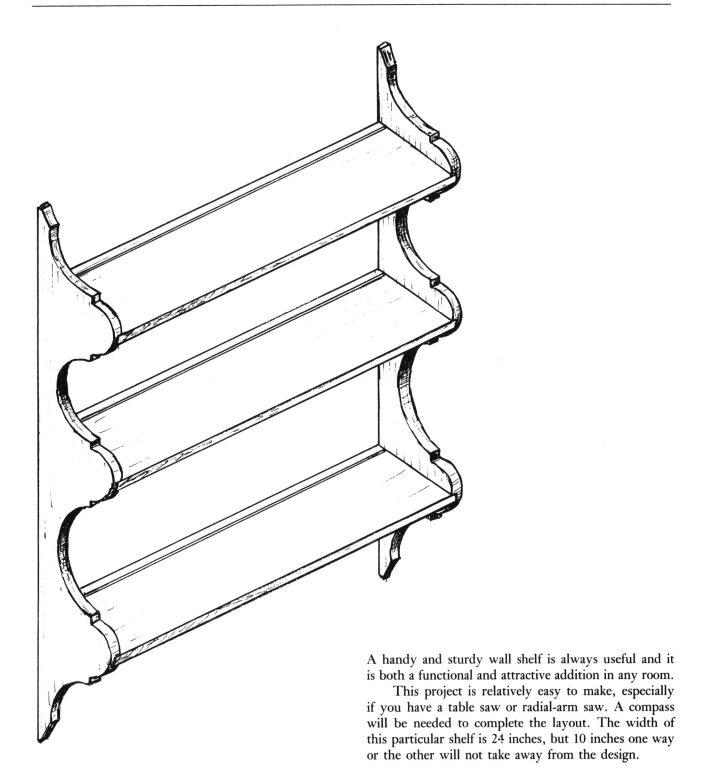

A handy and sturdy wall shelf is always useful and it is both a functional and attractive addition in any room.

This project is relatively easy to make, especially if you have a table saw or radial-arm saw. A compass will be needed to complete the layout. The width of this particular shelf is 24 inches, but 10 inches one way or the other will not take away from the design.

MATERIALS

1 1- by 6-inch by 12-foot #2 pine board
18 8d finish nails
4 7/16-inch-diameter plugs
Wood glue
Water putty
Sandpaper, medium and fine
Steel wool, #0000 grade
Stain of your choice
Tung oil

CONSTRUCTION

Cut the 1- by 6-inch board into five lengths. Three 24-inch long pieces of part 2 and two 32-inch long pieces of part 1. The three shelves (part 2) should be completely sanded, but do not "round" corners or edges. The plate stop (¼- by ¼-inch groove) is optional. If you do not have a power saw, it can be omitted. In fact, the original model did not have it. Refer to the 32-inch sides of part 1. Cut to size and carefully measure to locate the three grooves for the three shelves. If you have a power saw this is a simple step. The groove width must match or be a bit smaller than the shelf thickness (a tight fit is needed). Use the dimensions provided to locate the grooves.

If you do not have a power saw, position the grooves and use a square to scribe two pencil lines across the board. These lines will represent the top and bottoms of each groove. Using a handsaw, saw on the *inside* of the two lines, making the sides of the groove to the exact width and approximately ¼ inch deep.

Use a hand chisel to cut out the groove. Chisel in from the sides and keep the groove as flat as possible.

The two sides must match each other, so keep this in mind as you proceed.

Using the center of each groove, locate and swing the three 1⅝-inch radius arcs. Locate and swing the two 2½-inch radius arcs. Locate and swing the two 3¾-inch radius arcs. Carefully line up the two boards and the six grooves. Nail them together in two places at the center of the two end grooves with thin finish nails. With the two boards nailed together, cut out, file, and sand the edges so that the edges of both ends match exactly. Drill the two 3/16-inch-diameter holes 1⅛ inch from the ends of each part, as shown on the detail drawing. Using a 7/16-inch-diameter drill, counterbore these four holes approximately ⅜ inch deep.

Carefully remove the three nails and sand all surfaces, taking care not to round the edges.

ASSEMBLY

Put the three shelves in place. This should be a snug fit. If the fit is too snug, sand the shelf ends to fit. Using three finish nails at each shelf end, nail the shelves to the side boards. Countersink the eighteen nails and fill with water putty.

FINISHING

Be sure to line up the front of the shelves (part 2) with the front of the sides (part 1). Resand all surfaces, steel-wool, clean, and stain the entire project. Add tung oil to suit and hang.

After using the required screws to secure the shelves to the wall, insert the four 7/16-inch-diameter roundhead plugs to hide the wall screws. (These plugs should be stained to match shelves.)

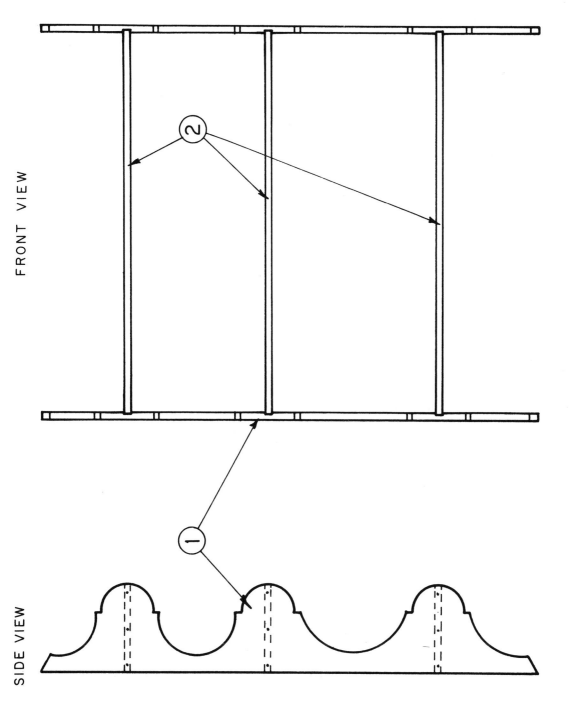

FRONT VIEW

SIDE VIEW

ASSEMBLY

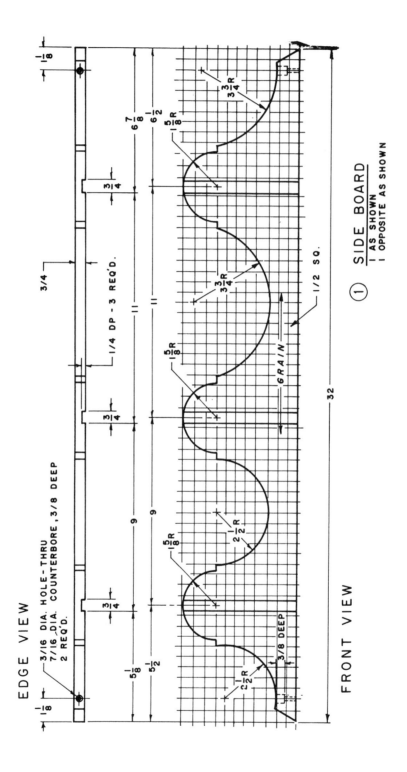

EDGE VIEW

FRONT VIEW

SIDE BOARD
1 AS SHOWN
1 OPPOSITE AS SHOWN

①

FRONT VIEW

END VIEW

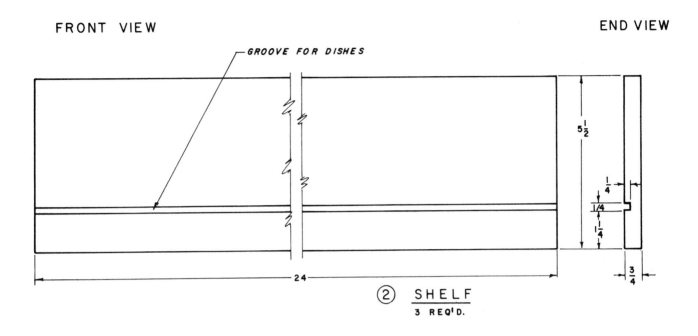

GROOVE FOR DISHES

24

$5\frac{1}{2}$

$\frac{1}{4}$

$\frac{1}{4}$

$1\frac{1}{4}$

$\frac{3}{4}$

② <u>SHELF</u>
3 REQ'D.

Eighteenth-Century
Pipe Holder

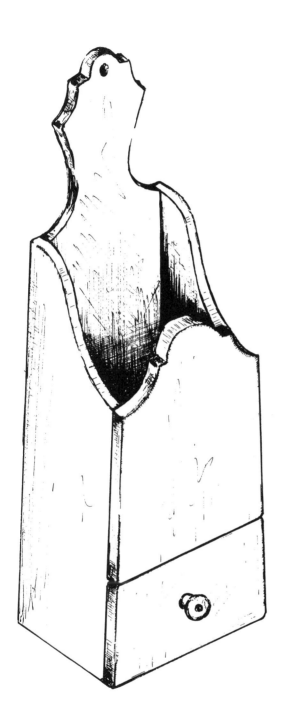

This project adds warmth to any Early American setting. Since it was very popular around the years 1745 to 1790, there are not many originals still in existence. The pipe box was used to hold and protect the long clay church warden pipes. The drawer was originally used for tobacco. Today, the pipe box makes an excellent planter or candle holder.

This unique original design has slightly tapered sides, which makes construction, especially for the drawer, a bit more difficult, but very different and worth the effort. Many original pipe boxes were constructed of cherry and some used dovetail construction.

MATERIALS

1 ⅜- by 6-inch by 6 foot #2 pine board
1 1- by 4- by 6-inch #2 pine board
1 ½- to ¾-inch diameter white glass drawer pull, with brass screw
Wood glue
Water putty
Sandpaper, medium and fine
Steel wool, #0000 grade
Stain of your choice
Tung oil

CONSTRUCTION

The tapered front creates assembly problems. Therefore it is important that you carefully study all detail drawings before starting. Notice that the drawer is illustrated as a subassembly (part 4) by itself, with five parts making up the completed drawer subassembly. Some "fitting" and sanding may have to be done in order to make the drawer fit and slide correctly.

In order to assure correct assembly follow the procedure closely. Carefully lay out and cut out the back panel (part 1). Both sides of the center line must match, so care must be taken in laying out the taper. Lay out and cut out the front panel (part 2). Look for an interesting knot or grain to highlight the pipe holder. It is suggested that the sides or part 2 be made approximately ⅟₃₂ inch oversize so you can sand down to size after assembly. Lay out and cut out two identical side panels (part 3). The brace (part 9) and bottom (part 10) should be cut from the remaining wood. You might wish to cut those two parts ⅟₁₆ inch or so longer than the 4⅝- and 4⅞-inch lengths noted. Sand all tops, bottoms, and edges of all parts. Do not "round" any edges at this time.

ASSEMBLY

Glue the two side panels (part 2) in place on back panel (part 1). Be sure to glue parts 9 and 10 in place before assembling the front panel (part 2). If the front panel was made ⅟₃₂ inch larger, as suggested, it may overlap the side panels. This is perfectly all right. After glue hardens, sand all surfaces, keeping all edges square at this time. Sand the front panel (part 2) to fit the side panels (part 3). Set the main assembly aside and make the drawer assembly.

For the beginner (and sometimes the advanced) woodworker, a drawer assembly is "tricky" to say the least. With an 8-degree taper, it really can be difficult. Carefully lay out and make all cuts, as noted on the drawer front (part 5).

Again I suggest that all outside dimensions be made ⅟₃₂ inch larger than noted so that the drawer front can be sanded to fit main assembly. Cut out identical drawer sides (part 6) according to the detail plan. Note that the sides are constructed from ⅜ inch thick materials.

Cut out the drawer back (part 7) from ¼-inch stock. If you have a table saw, the 2¾-inch-high back can be cut ¼ inch thick from ⅝-inch-thick stock.

ASSEMBLY

Cut out the drawer bottom (part 8) and sand all drawer parts. Using the drawer assembly (part 4), assemble the drawer to check all parts fit correctly. Cut or sand to make all parts fit correctly. If assembly fits correctly, glue all parts together, except the drawer bottom (part 8). The bottom should fit loosely and not be glued in place. This is a standard procedure to allow for expansion. Use two or three large rubber bands to hold assembly while glue is setting.

After the glue sets, sand all edges and fit the drawer assembly into the main assembly. The draw front should overlap a little over the main assembly. Sand in place to line up with the main assembly. Check to see that the drawer slides freely and that the lip on part 7 holds the drawer from falling out.

With the drawer in place, "round" all front surfaces, as noted on the assembly drawing. "Round" the top edges of part 1 and blend (round) the front and side edges of parts 2 and 3 to suit. Try to achieve that two-hundred-year-old worn look. Sand all surfaces, "distress," and steel-wool. Add stain, and, to achieve that real old effect, take a tube of burnt umber oil paint and add color to the edges. Fade color into original stain to suit your taste.

FRONT VIEW   SIDE VIEW

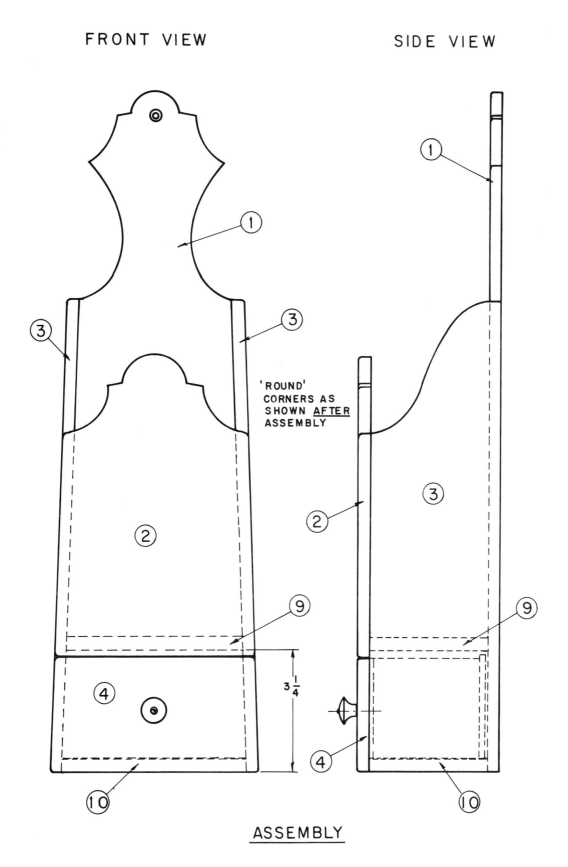

'ROUND'
CORNERS AS
SHOWN <u>AFTER</u>
ASSEMBLY

$3\frac{1}{4}$

ASSEMBLY

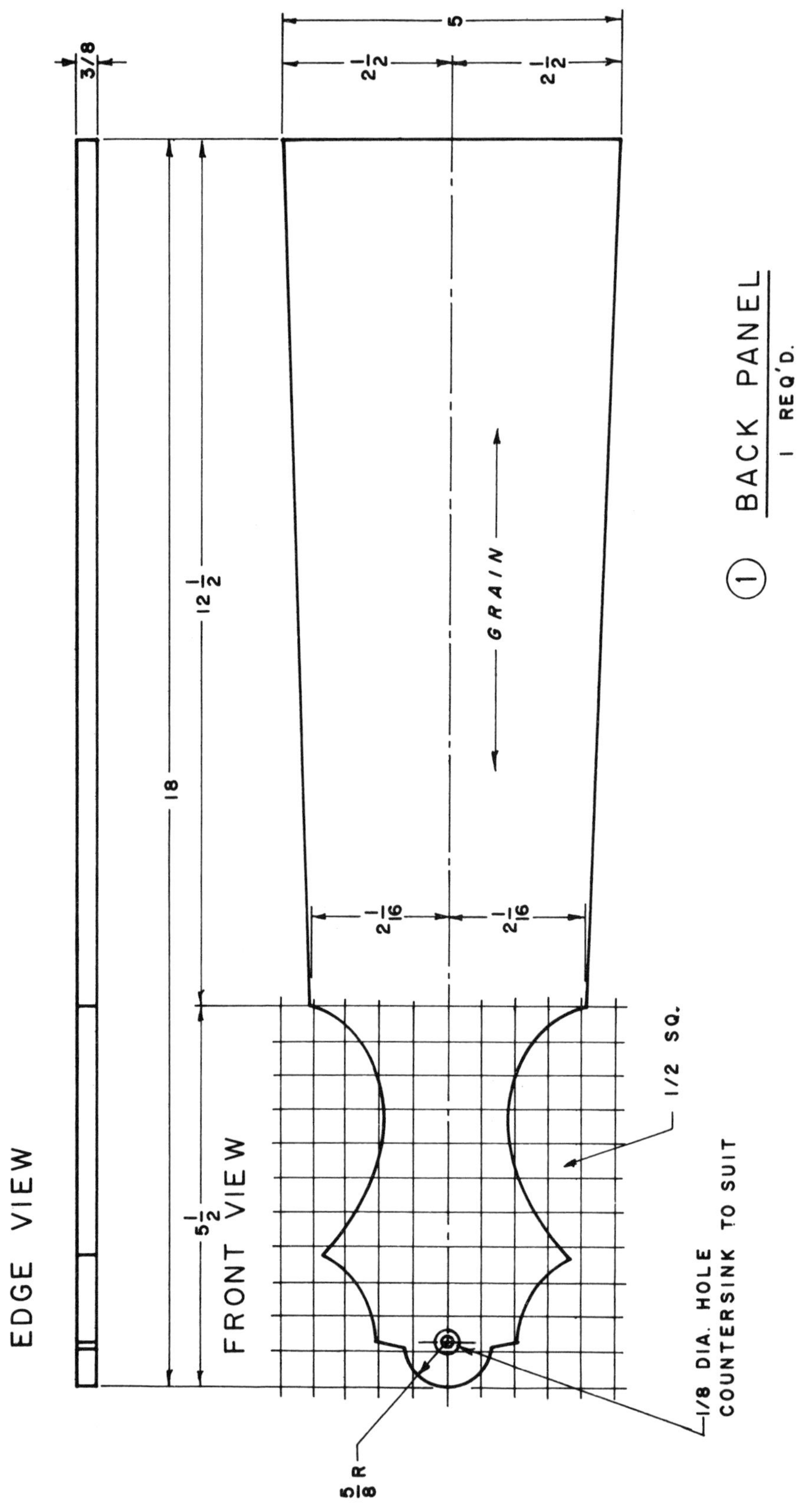

EDGE VIEW

FRONT VIEW

3/8

18

$12\frac{1}{2}$

$5\frac{1}{2}$

5

$2\frac{1}{2}$

$2\frac{1}{2}$

$2\frac{1}{16}$

$2\frac{1}{16}$

— GRAIN —

1/2 SQ.

1/8 DIA. HOLE
COUNTERSINK TO SUIT

$\frac{5}{8}$ R

① BACK PANEL
   1 REQ'D.

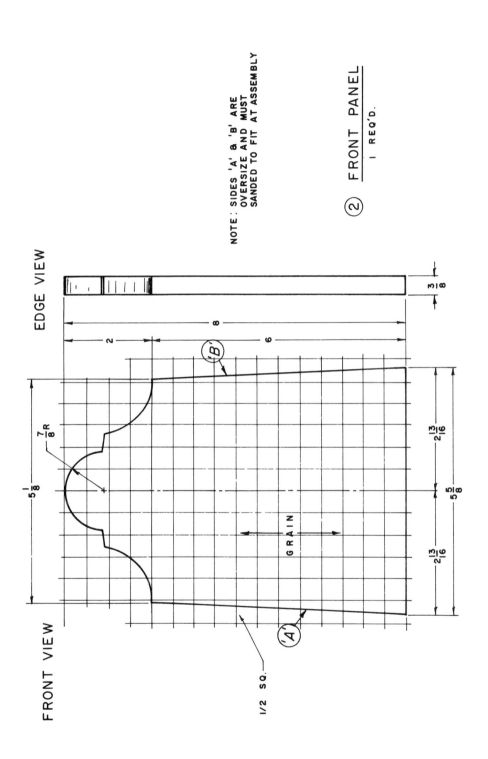

EDGE VIEW

FRONT VIEW

NOTE: SIDES 'A' & 'B' ARE
OVERSIZE AND MUST
SANDED TO FIT AT ASSEMBLY

② FRONT PANEL
1 REQ'D.

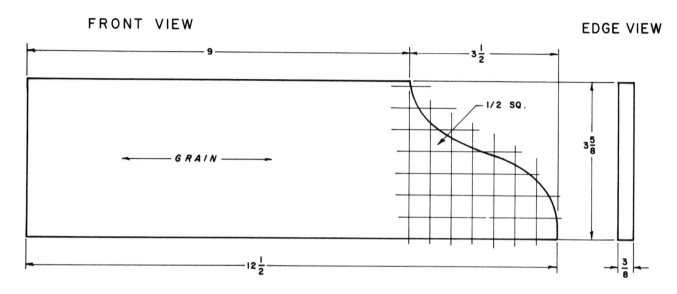

FRONT VIEW   EDGE VIEW

GRAIN

1/2 SQ.

③ <u>SIDE PANEL</u>
2 REQ'D.

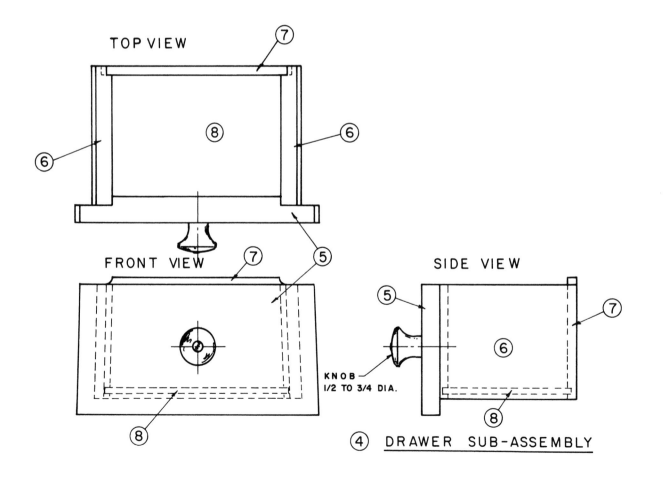

TOP VIEW

FRONT VIEW   SIDE VIEW

KNOB
1/2 TO 3/4 DIA.

④ <u>DRAWER SUB-ASSEMBLY</u>

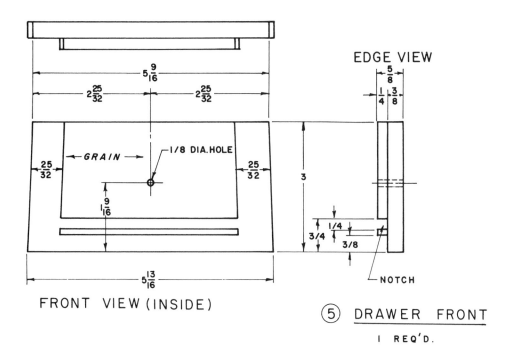

TOP VIEW

EDGE VIEW

FRONT VIEW (INSIDE)

⑤ DRAWER FRONT
1 REQ'D.

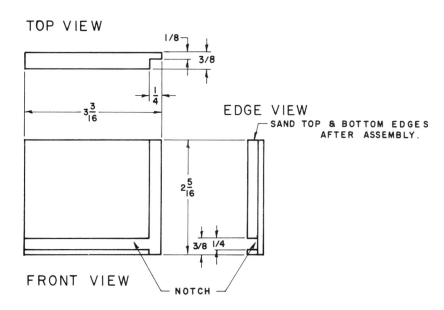

TOP VIEW

EDGE VIEW
SAND TOP & BOTTOM EDGES
AFTER ASSEMBLY.

FRONT VIEW

NOTCH

⑥ DRAWER SIDES
1 REQ'D. AS SHOWN
1 REQ'D. OPPOSITE AS SHOWN

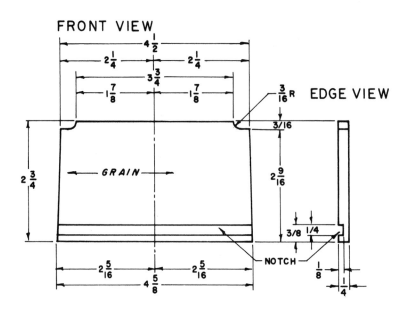

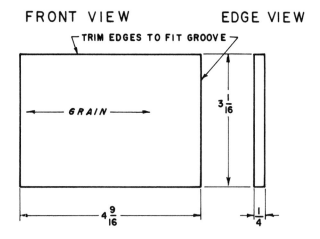

FRONT VIEW   EDGE VIEW

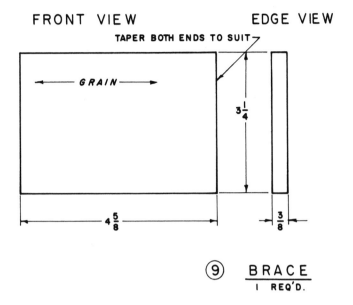

⑨   <u>BRACE</u>

I REQ'D.

FRONT VIEW   EDGE VIEW

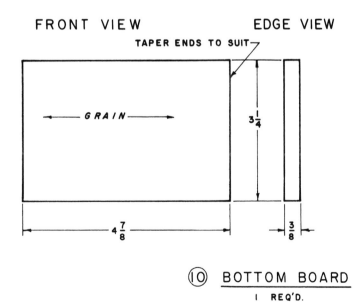

⑩   <u>BOTTOM BOARD</u>

I REQ'D.

Pennsylvania Dutch
Child's Bench

This unique design is a copy of an old child's bench from the Pennsylvania area. The original was painted with a design painted on the top portion of the ends. This project would lend itself to using original milk paint and if you are capable, tole a design on the ends.

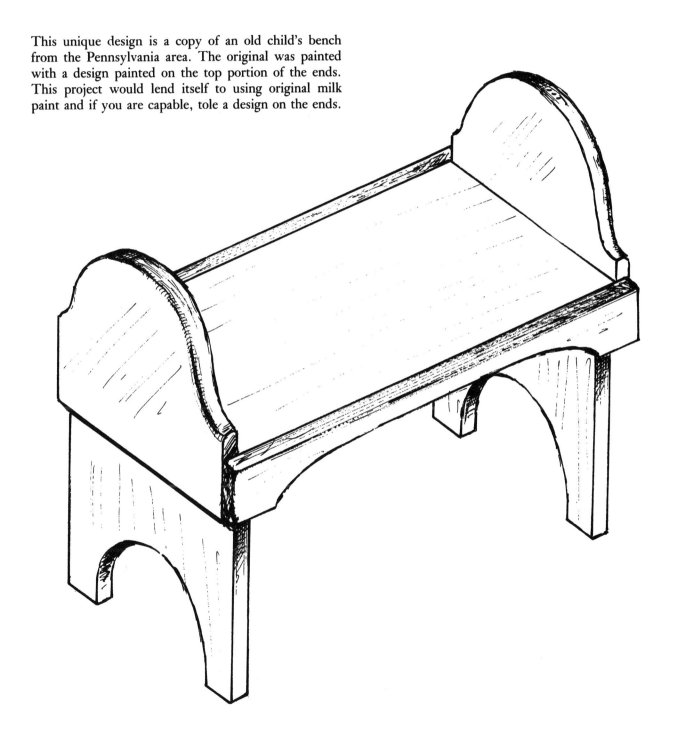

MATERIALS

1 1- by 12-inch by 6-foot #2 pine board
1 1- by 3-inch by 6-foot #2 pine board
40 8d finish nails
Wood glue
Water putty
Sandpaper, medium and fine
Steel wool, #0000 grade
Stain of your choice
Tung oil

CONSTRUCTION

In the event that 1- by 12-inch-size wood is not available, 1- by 10-inch-size wood could be substituted by cutting down the width of parts 1 and 2.

Lay out and cut out parts 1, 2, and 4. Note the direction of grain of each part. The top part 1 should be "rounded," as indicated on the detailed plan. Carefully make the 1/8- by 3/4-inch groove in part 1. This must fit tightly with part 4. Sand all edges and surfaces smoothly. Remember that parts 1 and 2 are made in pairs and must match each other exactly.

Lay out and cut out the two side supports (part 3). Cut parts 5 and 6 and sand all sides and edges.

ASSEMBLY

Glue and nail part 6 to the bottom end (part 2). Line up the edges and sand with a sanding block so as not to "round" any corners. Glue and nail the two top ends together with seat (part 4) and two side supports (part 3). Be sure to maintain 90-degree angles between all parts. Countersink all nails so they will not show in this project. Nailing straight down and through the seat (part 4) and about 1/4 inch away from the top ends (part 1), put three nails for each end directly into bottom ends (part 2). Do not forget to add glue to all surfaces before assembling. Glue part 5 in place to hide the three nails. Putting two or three nails through part 2 into part 1 (from the inside) will help make the assembly a little stronger, also.

FINISHING

The bench is now ready to be sanded. Use a sanding block to start and square all assembled corners. "Distress" to suit to add "those years of wear." Finish sanding with fine sandpaper and steel wool. Stain and finish. If you plan to paint the bench with milk paint, add two coats of tung oil first as an undercoat. Steel-wool between each coat of tung oil and before applying the milk paint.

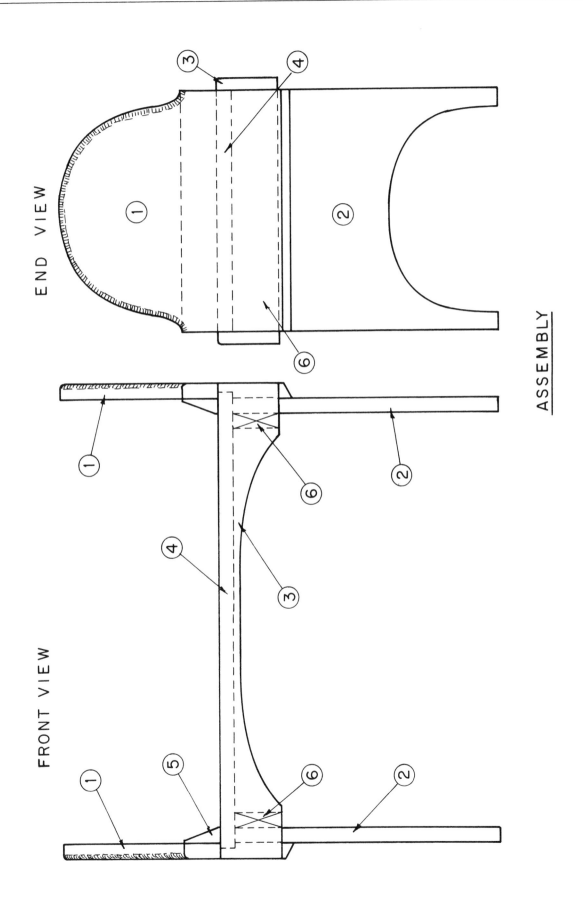

ASSEMBLY

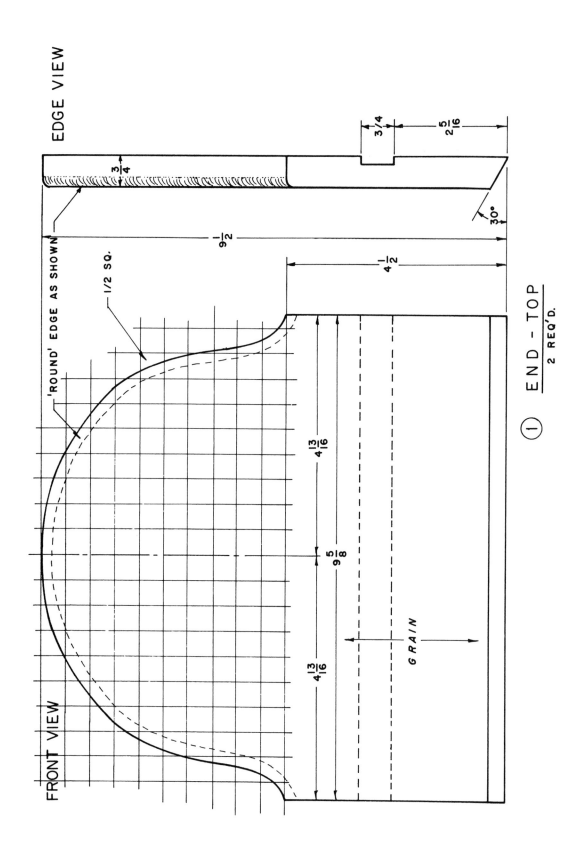

EDGE VIEW

3/4

2 5/16

3/4

9 1/2

'ROUND' EDGE AS SHOWN

1/2 SQ.

4 1/2

30°

4 13/16

9 5/8

4 13/16

GRAIN

FRONT VIEW

① END - TOP
2 REQ'D.

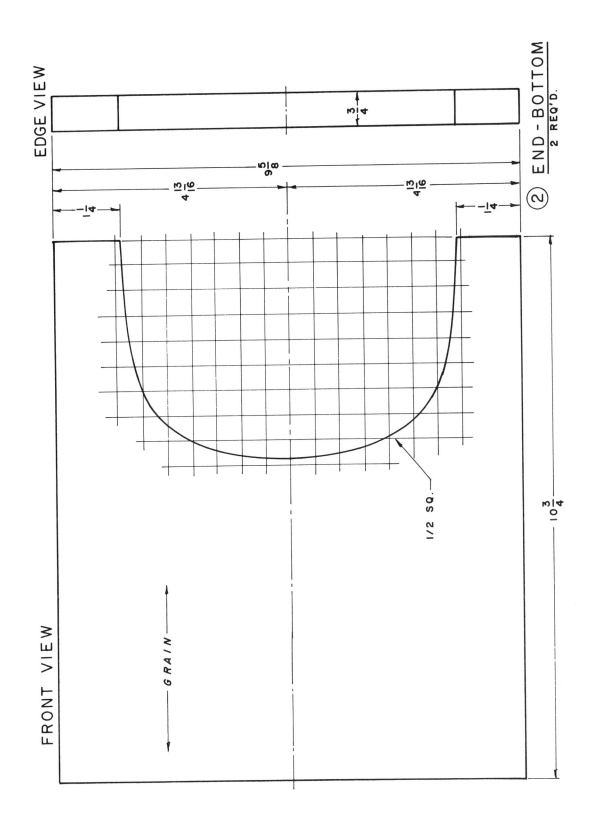

EDGE VIEW

FRONT VIEW

← GRAIN →

$9\frac{5}{8}$

$4\frac{13}{16}$

$4\frac{13}{16}$

$1\frac{1}{4}$

$1\frac{1}{4}$

$\frac{3}{4}$

$10\frac{3}{4}$

1/2 SQ.

② END - BOTTOM
2 REQ'D.

FRONT VIEW

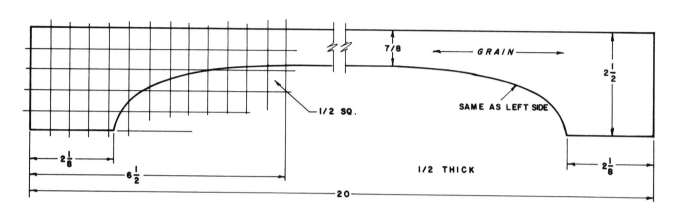

GRAIN

7/8

2½

1/2 SQ.

SAME AS LEFT SIDE

1/2 THICK

2⅛

6½

2⅛

20

③ SIDE SUPPORT
2 REQ'D.

FRONT VIEW

EDGE VIEW

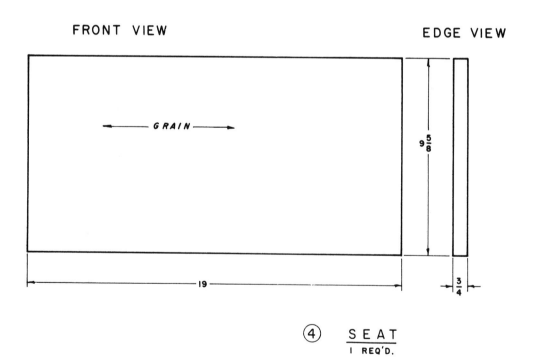

GRAIN

9⅝

19

¾

④ SEAT
1 REQ'D.

FRONT VIEW

END VIEW

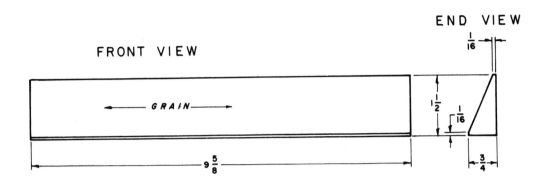

⑤ TOP BRACE

2 REQ'D.

FRONT VIEW

END VIEW

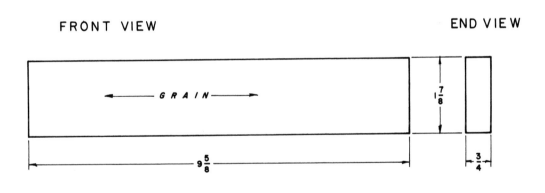

⑥ BOTTOM BRACE

2 REQ'D.

Six-Board Blanket Chest

A "six-board" blanket chest is exactly that—a chest made of six boards with a hinged top. These date back to the colonial days of our country, and many date as far back as the Pilgrims. While many had usable drawers, others had false drawers on the face of the box section. Many antique chests were painted and decorated with folk art. The original blanket chests used the old cotter-pin-type hinges. This particular blanket chest was found in Wakefield, Rhode Island.

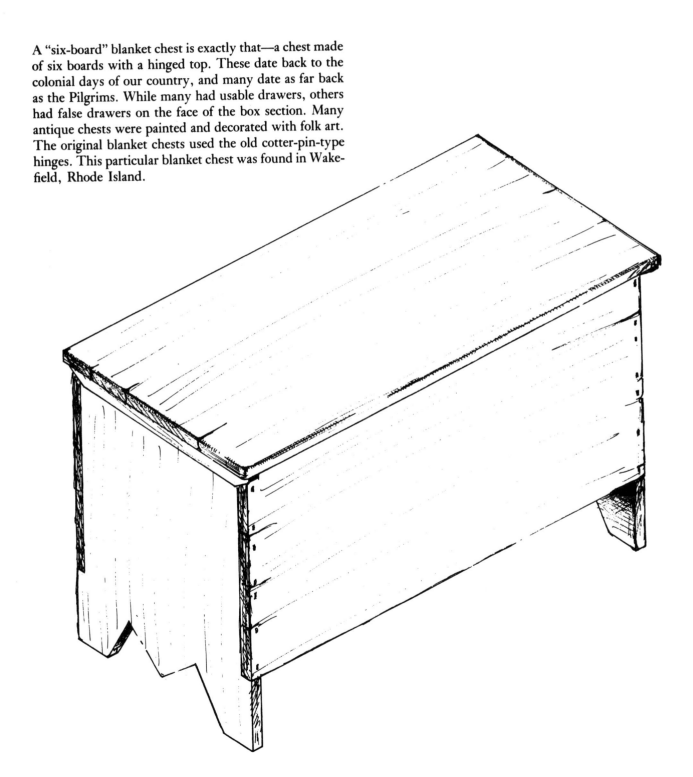

MATERIALS

2 1- by 10-inch by 16-foot (or 4 1- by 10-inch by 8-foot) #2 pine boards
1 1- by 2-inch by 3-foot #2 pine board
42 8d fine-finish nails (antique-cut style)
2 2-inch hinges (old style, if possible)
Wood glue
Water putty
Sandpaper, medium and fine
Steel wool, #0000 grade
Stain of your choice
Tung oil

CONSTRUCTION

Extra wide boards, such as those originally used on blanket chests, are very hard to find today. To obtain the wide board effect you must glue two 10-inch-wide boards together. Thus, before starting, plane one edge of each board so as to have a smooth, tight-fitting surface to glue the boards together. Normally, a power jointer would be used. But for this project, if care is taken, the plane will work almost as well.

Add glue to the edges and clamp tightly for a day or so. If you do not have clamps, wedge the two boards as tightly as possible. Wipe off any excess glue on both sides. After a day or so, remove clamps and, with the plane adjusted to a fine cut, plane the top and bottom surfaces. This will produce wavy surfaces much like those on an original chest. In fact, *try* to make the surfaces slightly wavy. Sand the entire surfaces, but do not try to remove the imperfect surface. This wavy surface will give your blanket chest that authentic look.

Using a square, mark off the approximate 18½-inch-wide boards you have just made into the following sizes: Two 23-inch-long ends (part 1), two 36-inch-long front/back (part 2), one 35-inch-long bottom (part 3), one 38-inch-long top (part 4).

It is important that these cuts are exactly 90 degrees. Sand the cut ends smooth.

Carefully study the detail drawing of the ends (part 1). Measure and make the ¾-inch groove across the boards. Cut the two ¾-inch-wide notches from the front and back sides, as shown. Take care to end the notch at the bottom of the groove, as shown. This is very important so that everything will be in line. Cut out the bottom legs or design, using the given dimensions.

The front/back (part 2) and bottom board (part 3) are already completed. Carefully using the plane, "round" the edges, approximately as shown. Do the ends (cross-grain) first. Be careful here not to "chip" out near the corner. From the 1- by 2-inch board cut two braces (part 5), sand, and "round" per the detail drawing.

ASSEMBLY

Glue and nail the bottom (part 3) to the two ends (part 1). Place nails about 4 or 5 inches apart. Don't try to hide the old nails, as they usually showed in the original pieces. Glue and nail the front and back boards in place. Don't be surprised if the front and back boards (part 2) overlap the ends a bit. This is to ensure that, in the event the notches in the ends (part 1) are not the correct depth, there will be enough material. Sand off any excess later. Take care that all angles are square (90 degrees). This is important! Again, do not try to hide the nails. Nail along the bottoms of the front and rear into part 3. Place nails 8 to 10 inches apart. Do not put the nails too close to the edge of the front/rear boards, as they might split the wood. Wipe excess glue off and recheck for "squareness."

Place top (part 4) on chest exactly where it is to go. Notice that the top is flush with the back board and does not overhang at the back—only in front and sides. With the top in place, draw a line along the two outside ends to locate where the braces (part 5) will be located. Remove and turn over. Glue and nail just outside the two lines, so braces do not "bind," when top is closed.

Position the two hinges approximately 8 inches in from the ends. Mark their location with a pencil and carefully, using a chisel, make a ¹⁄₁₆-inch (or so) notch out of the top edge of the back board (part 2) where the hinges will be set. Replace the top and screw the hinges to the top board. It is best to lay the chest on its side to do this. Be careful to position the top board so that the braces will clear the ends.

FINISHING

Using a block sander, sand all corners smooth and sharp. If the front/rear boards (part 2) overhang a bit, sand until flush with the end boards. Sand the top edges of inside of parts 1 and 2. "Round" the inside design of the legs of the ends (part 1). Because blanket chests received a lot of hard use, do not be afraid to really "distress" all sides. "Round" the edges and ends to simulate "wear" and add "scratches." As blanket chests were never finished inside, do not stain the interior of your chest. Sand and add a light coat of tung oil with a bit of burnt umber mixed. This adds that aged effect to your chest.

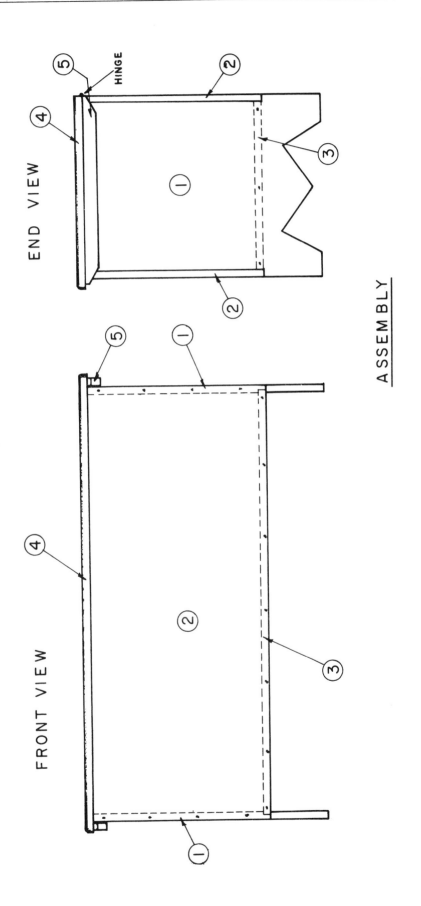

END VIEW

FRONT VIEW

ASSEMBLY

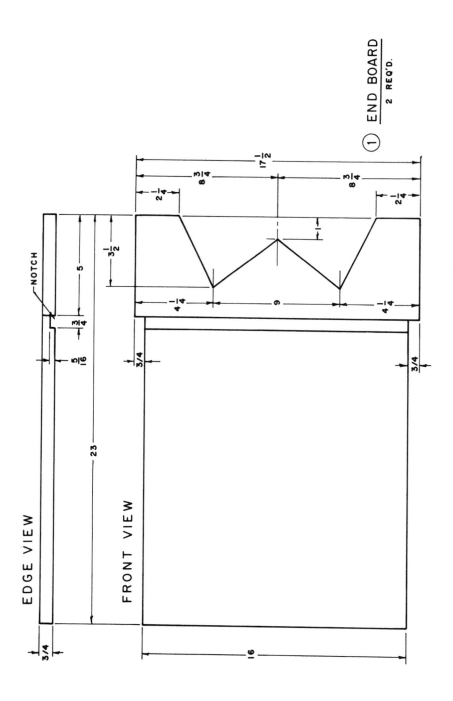

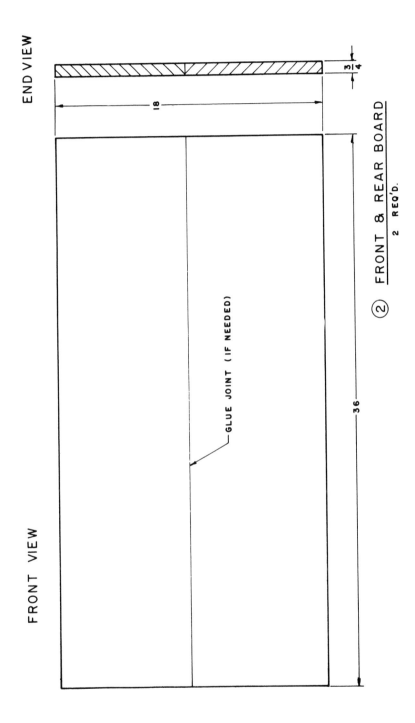

END VIEW

FRONT VIEW

18

3/4

GLUE JOINT (IF NEEDED)

36

② FRONT & REAR BOARD
2 REQ'D.

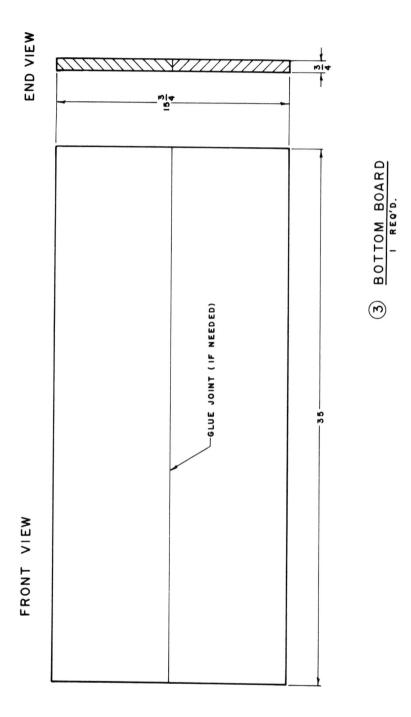

END VIEW

15¾

¾

FRONT VIEW

GLUE JOINT (IF NEEDED)

35

③ BOTTOM BOARD
1 REQ'D.

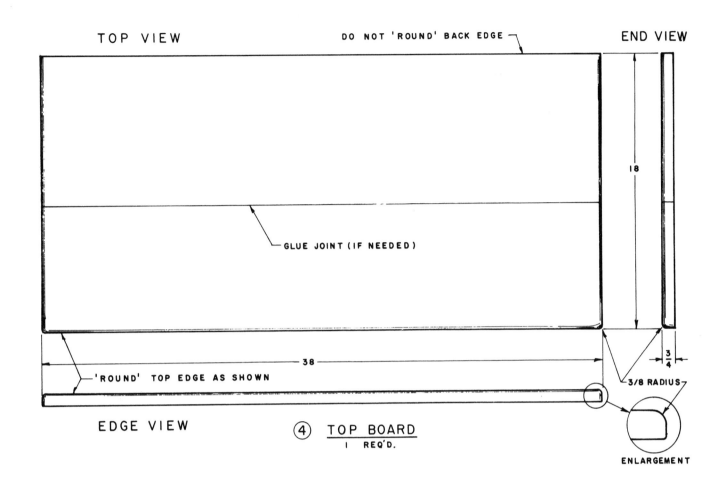

TOP VIEW

DO NOT 'ROUND' BACK EDGE

END VIEW

18

GLUE JOINT (IF NEEDED)

38

3/4

'ROUND' TOP EDGE AS SHOWN

EDGE VIEW

3/8 RADIUS

ENLARGEMENT

④ TOP BOARD
1 REQ'D.

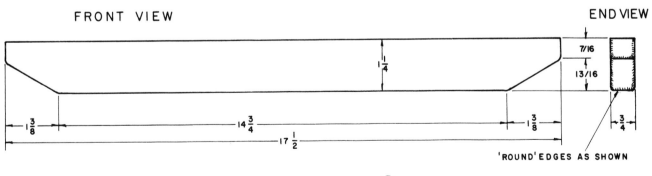

FRONT VIEW

END VIEW

$1\frac{1}{4}$

7/16

13/16

$1\frac{3}{8}$

$14\frac{3}{4}$

$1\frac{3}{8}$

$17\frac{1}{2}$

3/4

'ROUND' EDGES AS SHOWN

⑤ LID BRACE
2 REQ'D.

Standing Cupboard

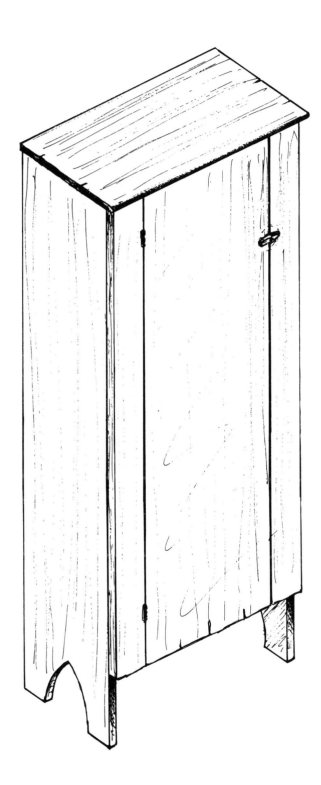

This cupboard is simple to make and will add charm to any room. It is useful for storing those odds and ends for which you never seem to have a spot. The proportions are especially pleasing to the eye and will be quite the conversation piece.

This particular design was taken from a crudely built original, which was found in northern Vermont. These cupboards were popular in 1800 or so and ranged in height from 2 to 5 feet. This design features the original simple bootjack base.

MATERIALS

1 1- by 10-inch by 8-foot #2 pine board
1 1- by 4-inch by 8-foot #2 pine board
1 1- by 10-inch by 6-foot #2 pine board
1 1- by 14-inch by 4-foot #2 pine board
1 ½- by 12- by 20-inch #2 pine board
1 1- by 4(5 or 6)-inch by 4-foot #2 pine board
2 hinges, 2 inches
50 8d fine-finish nails (antique-cut style)
1 #8 round-head screw, 1 inch long
Wood glue
Water putty
Sandpaper, medium and fine
Steel wool, #0000 grade
Stain of your choice
Tung oil

CONSTRUCTION

Carefully measure and locate all ¼- by ¾-inch grooves. Use a square and cut inside the ¾-inch-wide grooves. Chisel all grooves to ¼-inch depth, as shown. If you have a radial-arm saw, this process is very easy.

Important: Make one side, as shown. The other side is a "mirror" image of the first. Do not make both the same. Lay out and cut the "bootjack" ends.

Measure and cut to size the two front side boards (part 2). Measure and cut to size the four shelves (part 4). Measure and cut to size the door (part 5). If a 12-inch board is hard to find, glue two boards together to obtain the correct width. Try to find boards with interesting knots and grain structure. Position and add the two braces, cut from scrap, as shown on the detail drawing. Cut the ½-inch-thick board to size and "round" front of board, as shown.

The latch (part 8) is cut and carved from scrap. Any shape of this approximate size will do. The back (part 3) is made from scrap, any size, and glued together. Cut and "square" to size after glue sets and dries. Plane and sand both sides. Keep edges sharp and "square."

ASSEMBLY

Glue and nail the four shelves (part 4) together with the two side boards (part 1). Be sure everything is "square" or at 90-degree angles to each other. Let the nails show. Do not try to countersink them.

Glue and nail the glued-up back (part 3). This does not have to be a tight fit; ¹⁄₁₆ inch or so around all sides will be about right. Do not fill the spaces. Leave ¹⁄₁₆ inch of a space for expansion. Be sure that the top of the two sides (part 1) lines up with the top of the back (part 3). If it does not line up, check all work for square-

ness. Cut to fit, if necessary, but be sure it does line up.

Lay the stand on its back and position the door (part 5) approximately where it is to be located. Using four pieces of cardboard for spacers between the door and the two side boards (part 2), glue and nail the two front side boards (part 2) in place. Remove the cardboard and door. Be sure to leave the space between the door and the side boards. The side boards should overhang a bit on the sides. This overhang is acceptable, as it will be sanded to fit later. Check to see that the top of the front side boards (part 2) extend up to the top of the end boards (part 1). Nail and glue the top (part 6) in place. The back of the top must be flush with the back surface; the overhang of the top is only at the sides and the front. Be sure to add an extra nail through the top down into the side boards (part 2), as nothing supports the side boards except glue and these two nails.

To "hang" the door requires a little extra effort to achieve that "just right" fit. Measure 6 inches down from the left edge of the door and, using the hinge as a guide, scribe a line along the top and bottom of the hinge. Measure 6 inches up from the left edge of the door and again, using the hinge as a guide, scribe a line along the top and bottom of the hinge. With a sharp chisel, notch approximately ¹⁄₁₆ inch deep where the hinges will be located. Screw hinges in place on the door.

With the stand on its back, put the door in place approximately ¹⁄₁₆ inch down from the top. Mark the location of the top and bottom of the hinges on the left side board (part 2). Remove the door and carefully notch for the hinges. Care must be taken not to notch too deeply—just to the thickness of the hinge strap. Screw the door hinges into the two notches in the side board and check for clearance and fit. Locate the carved latch approximately 8 inches down the opposite side of the hinges. Locate the latch in from the edge of the front side board, approximately half the thickness of the latch. Attach latch in place using the 1-inch brass screw. (A washer under the latch may be needed.) To achieve that "old" look, place a piece of #100 sandpaper under the latch, facing the side board and door, and rotate the latch with the sandpaper in place. This will sand in a circle the exact size of the latch and give it that "worn" look (as if the latch had been turned for 150 years). "Distress" the complete assembly. Sand and finish sanding with the #0000 steel wool.

A light blue or yellow milk paint interior adds a lot to the cupboard. If you do paint the cupboard, be sure to tung oil all surfaces, inside and out before painting.

FRONT VIEW

SIDE VIEW

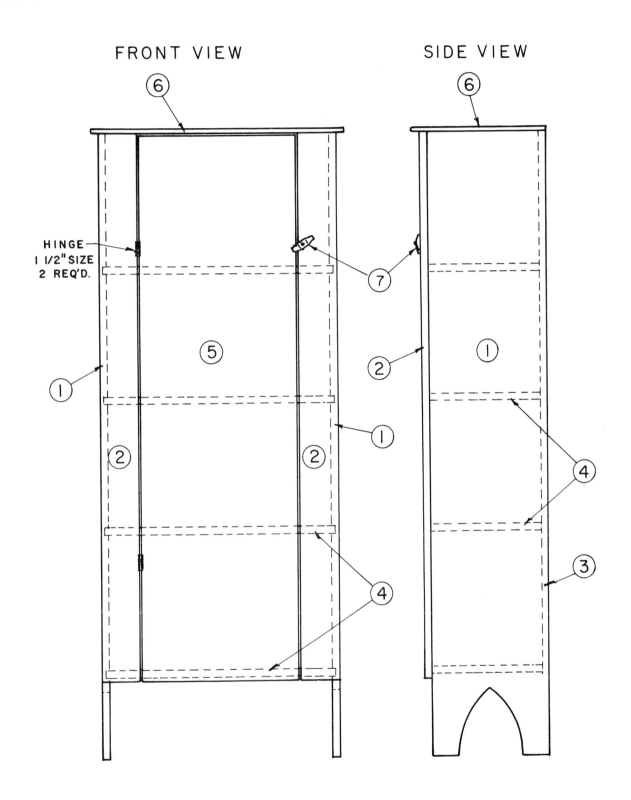

HINGE
1 1/2" SIZE
2 REQ'D.

ASSEMBLY

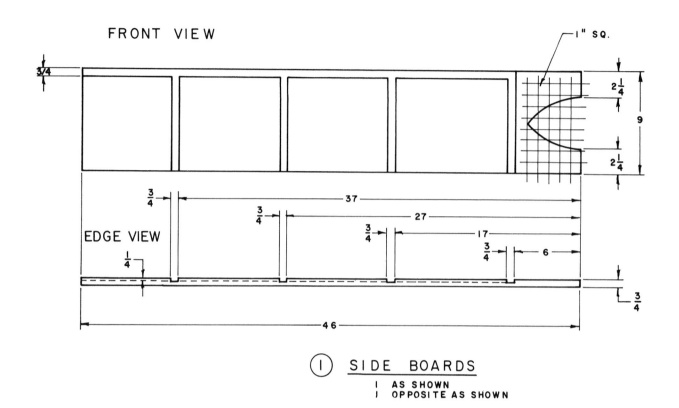

FRONT VIEW

EDGE VIEW

① SIDE BOARDS

1 AS SHOWN
1 OPPOSITE AS SHOWN

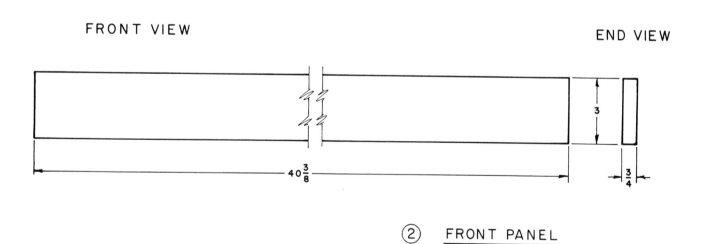

FRONT VIEW

END VIEW

② FRONT PANEL

2 REQ'D.

FRONT VIEW   END VIEW

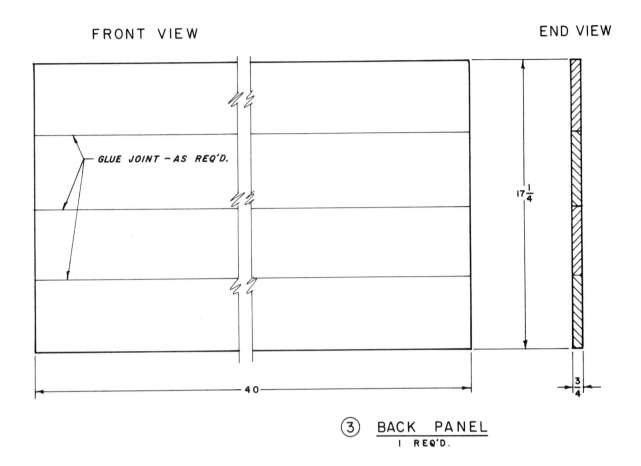

GLUE JOINT – AS REQ'D.

$17\frac{1}{4}$

40

$\frac{3}{4}$

③ <u>BACK PANEL</u>
<u>1 REQ'D.</u>

FRONT VIEW   END VIEW

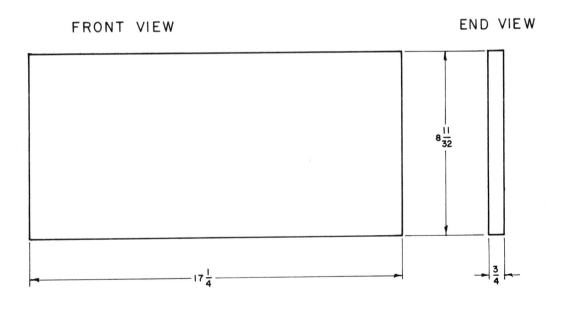

$8\frac{11}{32}$

$17\frac{1}{4}$

$\frac{3}{4}$

④ <u>S H E L F</u>
<u>4 REQ'D.</u>

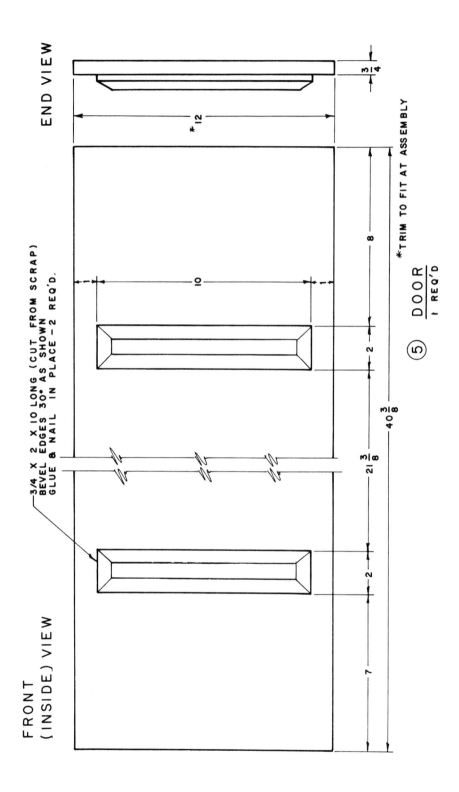

END VIEW

FRONT (INSIDE) VIEW

3/4 X 2 X 10 LONG (CUT FROM SCRAP)
BEVEL EDGES 30° AS SHOWN
GLUE & NAIL IN PLACE — 2 REQ'D.

*TRIM TO FIT AT ASSEMBLY

⑤ DOOR
1 REQ'D

FRONT VIEW

END VIEW

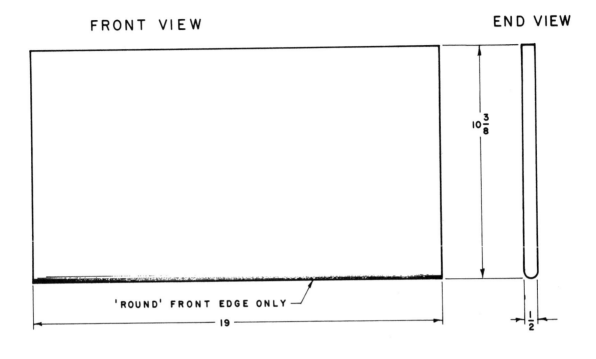

$10\frac{3}{8}$

19

'ROUND' FRONT EDGE ONLY

$\frac{1}{2}$

⑥ TOP BOARD

1 REQ'D.

1/8 DIA. HOLE - THRU

TOP VIEW

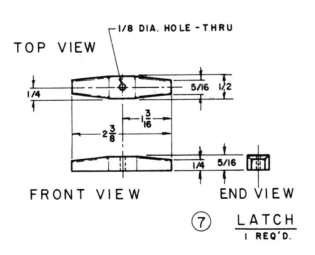

1/4

5/16 1/2

$1\frac{3}{16}$

$2\frac{3}{8}$

1/4 5/16

FRONT VIEW

END VIEW

⑦ LATCH

1 REQ'D.

Adjustable Candle Stand

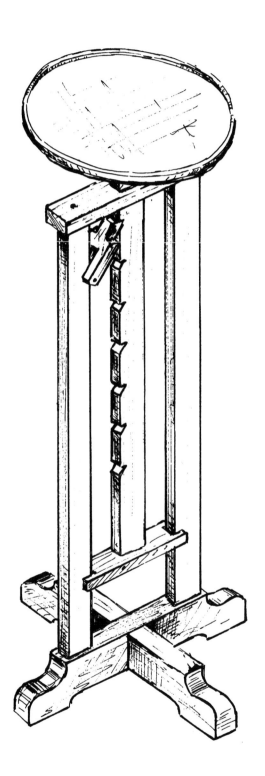

Simple, but ingenious, the adjustable candle stand compensated for the burning candle. As the candle shortened, the top was simply raised to keep the "light" at the same level. This simple project makes an interesting conversation piece and adds to any antique setting. Today, the stand can be utilized for many uses, in the event you no longer use candles for light.

MATERIALS

1 1- by 2-inch by 8-foot #2 pine board
1 ⁵⁄₄- by 3-inch by 2-foot #2 pine board
1 1- by 10- by 10-inch #2 pine board
12 10d finish nails
1 ³⁄₈- by 12-inch dowel
1 ¹⁄₈- by 2-inch dowel
2 #8 round-head brass screws, 1 inch long
Wood glue
Water putty
Sandpaper, medium and fine
Steel wool, #0000 grade
Stain of your choice
Tung oil

Note: A ⁵⁄₄ inch thick board measures about 1¼ inch thick.

CONSTRUCTION

Individual parts are quite simple to make, but assembly can be difficult. Study the assembly drawing before going too far.

Cut to size the adjusting arm (part 1). Add the eight notches and drill the two ³⁄₈-inch-diameter holes at each end, as shown. Cut to size the two main legs. Note only one has the ¹⁄₈-inch-diameter hole.

Using the ⁵⁄₄-inch-thick board (1 full inch thick), lay out and cut out the two feet (part 3). *Important:* Notice that one has the ¾- by ⅞-inch notch at the top (notch A) with the two ³⁄₈-inch-diameter holes, as shown on the detail plan. The other foot is the exact same size, but has the ¾- by ⅞-inch notch from underneath (notch B) and has no ³⁄₈-inch-diameter holes. Sand to fit the two notches so that the two feet fit tightly together. Cut and notch the guide (part 4), as shown. Be sure the two ¹⁹⁄₃₂- by ¹³⁄₁₆-inch slots on each end slide up and down the main legs. Cut, drill, and chisel out the ¹³⁄₁₆- by ¹¹⁄₁₆-inch rectangular hole on the top rail (part 5). Check to see that the adjusting arm (part 1) slides freely in the rectangular hole. Try to keep the four inside corners sharp.

Study the trigger (part 6) and carefully cut according to the detail drawing. Using a compass, mark out the ¾-inch-diameter top support (part 7) using a rasp. Form the edge on a 45-degree angle approximately as shown. Drill the ³⁄₈-inch-diameter hole. Refer to top (part 8). Using the compass, lay out the 9-inch diameter and cut out. If you have a router or saw attachment,

cut the ogee edge, as shown. Any edge, even a simple "rounded" edge, will do, if you have no power tools. A lip can be added to the top surface (see Figure 14-1) if you wish. The edge contour is limited to whatever tools you have to work with.

Sand all parts, as this is hard to sand after assembled. I suggest that you completely finish all parts at this time. You may also wish to add the stain now. Cut the ³⁄₈-inch dowel into six ¹⁵⁄₁₆-inch-long lengths. Glue the six dowels into the ends of the adjusting arm (part 1) and two main legs (part 2) and let set. Glue the two feet together. Check that they are at 90-degree angles to each other. Nail through from the bottom.

Glue the guide (part 4) to the adjusting arm and sand the dowel flush with the bottom of the guide. Add two nails from the bottom. Check to see that the dowels sticking out of the bottoms of the main legs (part 2) are not so long as to hold the legs away from the foot. If they are too long, drill the holes deeper. Glue the two main legs to the foot. Check for a snug fit where they join together. Check to see that one of the main legs has the ¹⁄₈-inch-diameter hole at the top end and in toward the center, according to the assembly drawing. Turn the work upside down and put two nails (each side) through the foot into the main legs (countersink). Be sure legs are at 90-degree angles to the feet. This is a very weak area so be sure the nails reach well up into the two main legs. Let glue set thoroughly, before going further.

Slide the adjusting arm (part 1) throught the top rail (part 5) and glue and nail the top support to the top of the legs. Glue top support (part 7) to the top adjusting arm (part 1). Insert trigger (part 6) in place with the ¹⁄₈-inch-diameter dowel. Check to see that the ¹⁄₈-inch-diameter holes in the trigger are loose so that the trigger moves freely. Check that the trigger fits fairly tightly and correctly into all eight notches. Also check to see that the adjusting arm (part 1) slides up and down without any binding. If there is any binding, simply slide the sandpaper between the mating parts and sand until parts move freely.

Extend the adjusting arm to full length. Turn assembly upside down and screw the top (part 8) with the two brass screws through the top support (part 7).

FINISHING

If you have not stained the stand before, stain and tung oil at this time.

FRONT VIEW

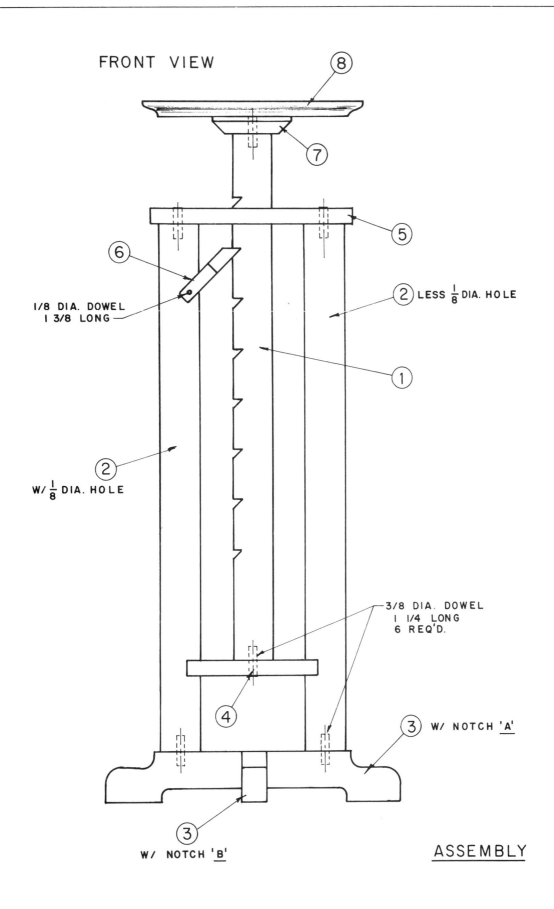

1/8 DIA. DOWEL
1 3/8 LONG

2 LESS $\frac{1}{8}$ DIA. HOLE

W/ $\frac{1}{8}$ DIA. HOLE

3/8 DIA. DOWEL
1 1/4 LONG
6 REQ'D.

3 W/ NOTCH 'A'

3

W/ NOTCH '<u>B</u>'

ASSEMBLY

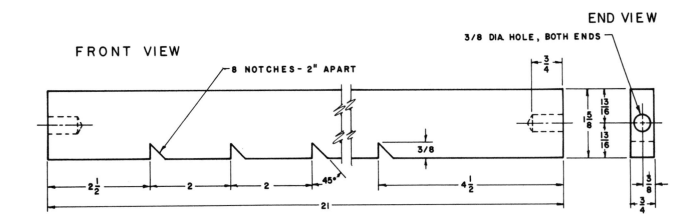

(1) ADJUSTING ARM
1 REQ'D.

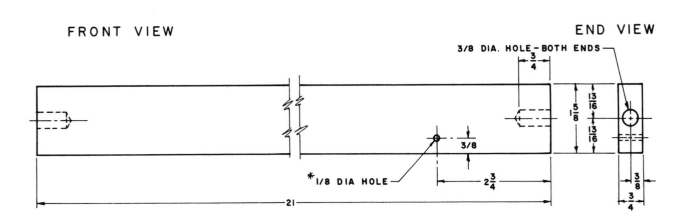

(2) MAIN LEG
1 AS SHOWN
*1 AS SHOWN MINUS 1/8" DIA. HOLE

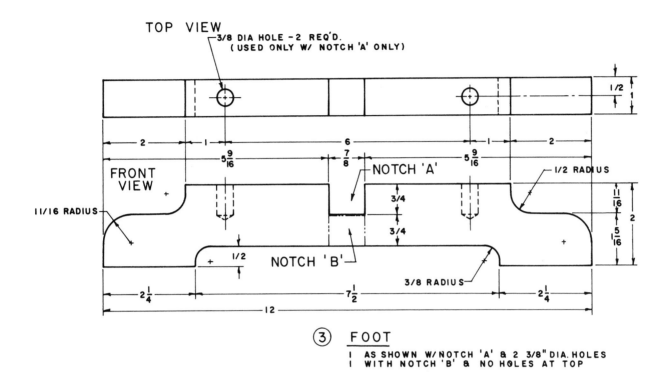

TOP VIEW

3/8 DIA HOLE - 2 REQ'D.
(USED ONLY W/ NOTCH 'A' ONLY)

FRONT VIEW

NOTCH 'A'

1/2 RADIUS

11/16 RADIUS

NOTCH 'B'

3/8 RADIUS

③ FOOT

1 AS SHOWN W/NOTCH 'A' & 2 3/8" DIA. HOLES
1 WITH NOTCH 'B' & NO HOLES AT TOP

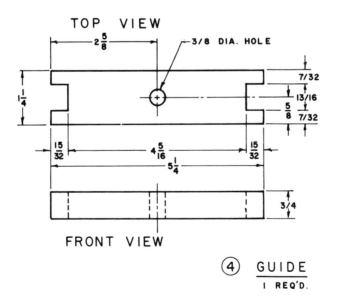

TOP VIEW

3/8 DIA. HOLE

FRONT VIEW

④ GUIDE

1 REQ'D.

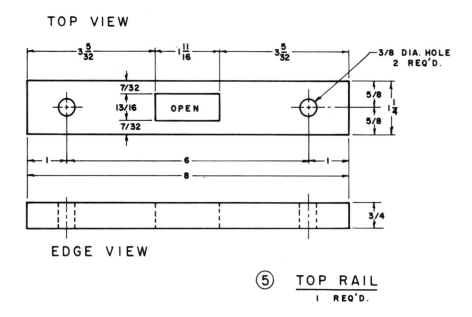

TOP VIEW

OPEN

EDGE VIEW

⑤ TOP RAIL
   1 REQ'D.

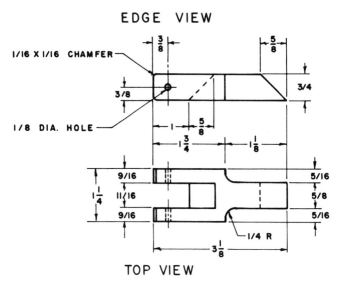

EDGE VIEW

1/16 X 1/16 CHAMFER

1/8 DIA. HOLE

TOP VIEW

⑥ TRIGGER
   1 REQ'D.

FRONT VIEW   SIDE VIEW

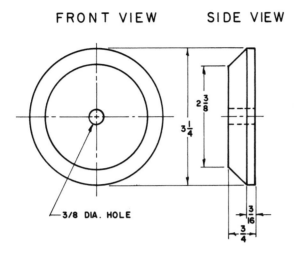

⑦ TOP SUPPORT
I REQ'D.

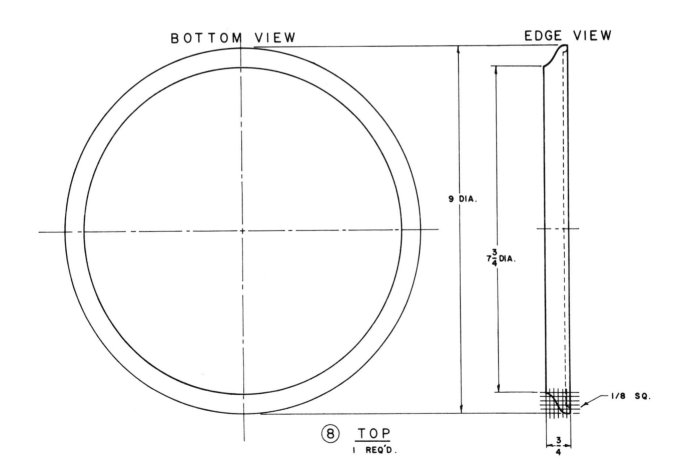

⑧ TOP
I REQ'D.

Hanging Book Shelf
With Drawers

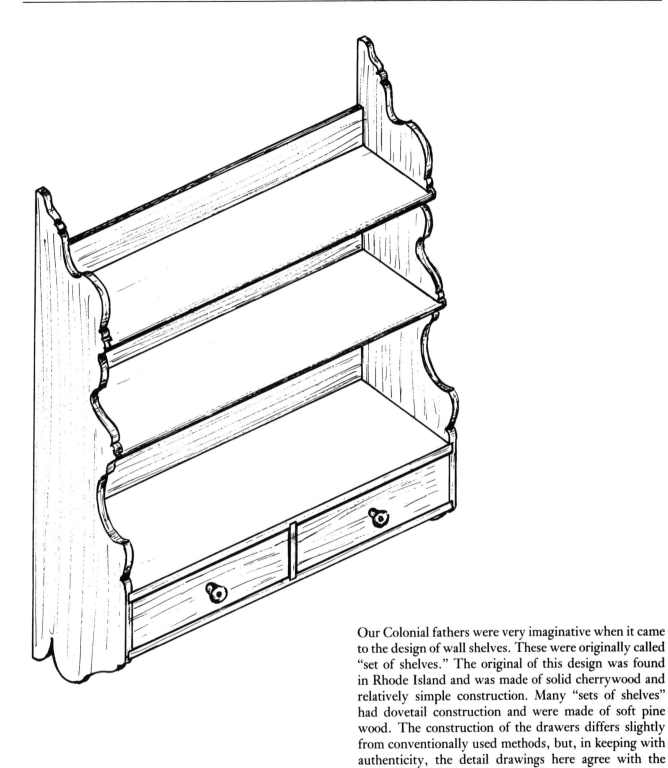

Our Colonial fathers were very imaginative when it came to the design of wall shelves. These were originally called "set of shelves." The original of this design was found in Rhode Island and was made of solid cherrywood and relatively simple construction. Many "sets of shelves" had dovetail construction and were made of soft pine wood. The construction of the drawers differs slightly from conventionally used methods, but, in keeping with authenticity, the detail drawings here agree with the original design.

MATERIALS

2 ½- by 8-inch by 8-foot #2 pine boards
1 ¼- by 4-inch by 8-foot #2 pine board
1 ⅜- by 4-inch by 6-foot #2 pine board
1 ⅜- by 8-inch by 2-foot #2 pine board
2 ¾-inch-diameter white glass drawer pulls, with brass
   screws
60 6d finish nails
24 nails, ½ inches long
Wood glue
Water putty
Sandpaper, medium and fine
Steel wool, #0000 grade
Stain of your choice
Tung oil
Lemon oil

CONSTRUCTION

Cut to overall size the two sides (part 1). Locate and, with a "square," draw the four ⅛-inch-deep by ½-inch-wide grooves across the board. Be sure both sides match exactly up to this point. Cut inside both lines down ⅛ inch deep and chisel the groove straight across the boards. Check that the ½-inch-thick stock wood fits tightly into the groove without "play." Starting from the cut grooves, lay out the design, using ½-inch squares for a guide wherever needed. Be sure the end of each groove lines up with the "round" design, as shown in the detail drawing. Make the rest of the design fit the grooves. Do not forget that the profile is reversed on the other one side.

Line up the back edge of both parts and the four grooves. Temporarily nail the two parts together with two finish nails, one nail through the center of the top grooves and the other nail through the center of the bottom grooves. Using a coping saw, rasp, file, and sandpaper. Finish the profile (front) edge together so that both sides will be identical. Remember that the grooves of both parts must be on the inside. Cut to size the four shelves (parts 2, 3, 4, and 5). Add rounded fronts with a rasp or plane, as indicated on the plan. The ⅛- by ¼-inch plate-groove does not have to be included if you do not have the equipment to make them.

Cut to size the four back boards (parts 6 and 7). In the event you could not cut out the ⅛- by ¼-inch grooves, part 7 should be cut to approximate 3¼ inches wide. It might be a good idea to cut the overall length to 23⅛ inches and to trim to exact size at assembly.

Cut the spacer (part 8) to size. Note the direction of grain.

ASSEMBLY

Check all parts to see that everything fits together. If all parts seem to be the correct size, start assembly. Add a small amount of glue inside the four grooves of the sides (part 1) and insert the four shelves in the correct order. Be sure everything is "square." Nail each shelf in place with three nails in each end. Cut and fit the four back boards. Glue at the ends and nail through the two sides to hold in place.

In order to have a grain pattern from the left drawer to the right drawer, study and select an interesting piece of wood for the drawer fronts (part 10). Cut board ⅜ by 3³⁄₁₆ by 22½ inches long. This will be the two drawer fronts. Take care to keep them in order so the grain patterns will flow from left to right. Choose the front side, turn the board, and cut the lower ⅛- by ³⁄₁₆-inch groove the entire length of the drawer fronts. Cut the two drawers apart (11³⁄₁₆ inches long each). Cut the notch at the two ends ¼ by ⁵⁄₁₆ inch, as shown. Locate and drill the ⅛-inch-diameter hole, according to the detail drawing. Keep the two drawer fronts in order so that the grain pattern will extend and flow across both drawers when completed.

Plane wood to approximately ⁵⁄₁₆ inch thick for the drawer sides (part 11) and drawer back or end (part 12). Cut parts 11 and 12 to size and notch according to detail drawings.

Plane a piece of wood 7¹⁄₁₂ by 22 inches to a thickness of ⁵⁄₁₆ inch. Cut to size (6¹³⁄₁₆ inch by 10⅞ inch) and cut the ³⁄₁₆ inch by ³⁄₁₆ inch "step" around all four sides of each piece, as illustrated in drawer bottom (plan 13). When assembling drawers, check to see that all parts fit together.

Glue and nail drawers together. Note that drawer bottom (part 13) is not nailed or glued and that the flat side is placed in the "up" position in the drawer assembly before it is put together. Sand all sides and edges. Install drawers in main assembly in the original order so that the grain pattern of the drawer fronts match. You may have to sand carefully and "custom-fit" each drawer. But, if you follow the dimensions fairly closely, the drawers should be approximately right. Sand/fit drawers until they slide freely and appear to have an equal space around the left, top, and right side of each.

Sand, steel-wool, and add stain. To achieve that antique appearance, add burnt umber oil paint in various spots to highlight the profile design of the front edges. Add tung oil to suit. This is a "formal" piece of furniture. Therefore, a high-gloss finish—four or five coats of tung oil—should be applied. Do not stain the insides of the drawers. Add the two ¾-inch diameter white glass draw pulls. To attach shelves to wall, screw through the back boards (part 6) in four places. Use lemon oil for polishing shelf after mounting to wall.

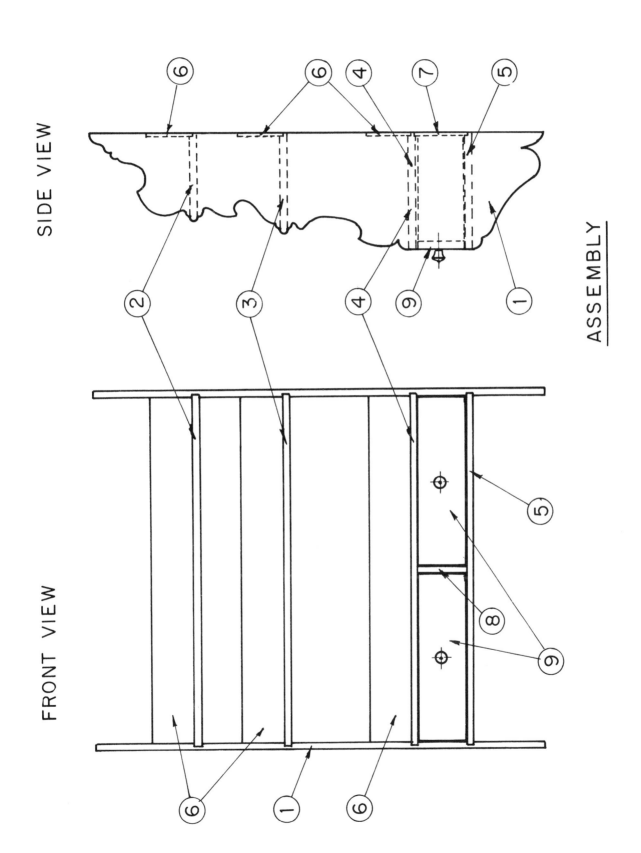

SIDE VIEW

ASSEMBLY

FRONT VIEW

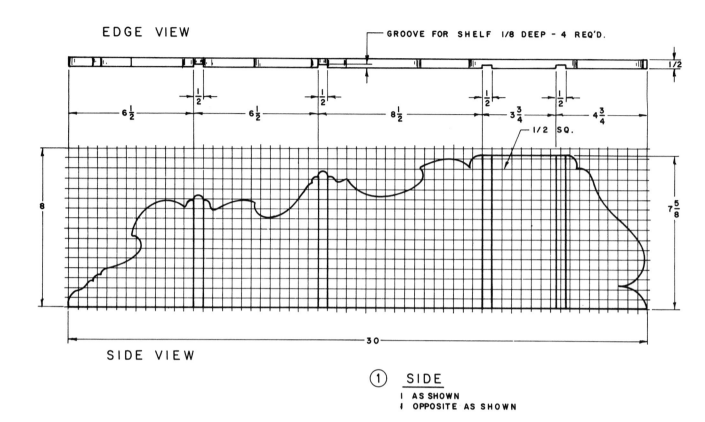

EDGE VIEW

GROOVE FOR SHELF 1/8 DEEP - 4 REQ'D.

1/2

6½   6½   8½   3¾   4¾

½   ½   ½   ½

1/2 SQ.

8

7⅝

30

SIDE VIEW

① SIDE
I AS SHOWN
I OPPOSITE AS SHOWN

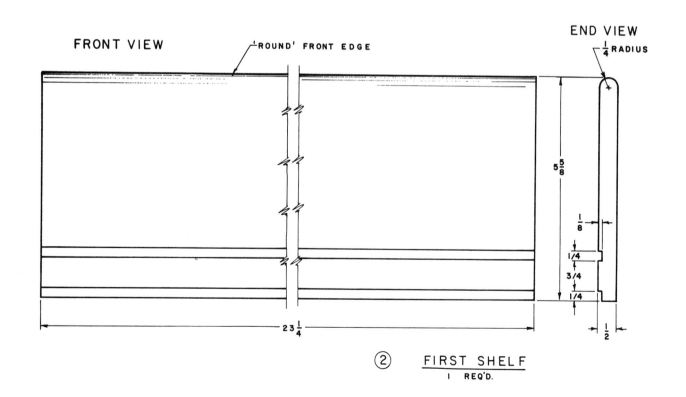

FRONT VIEW

'ROUND' FRONT EDGE

END VIEW

¼ RADIUS

5⅝

⅛

1/4

3/4

1/4

23¼

½

② FIRST SHELF
I REQ'D.

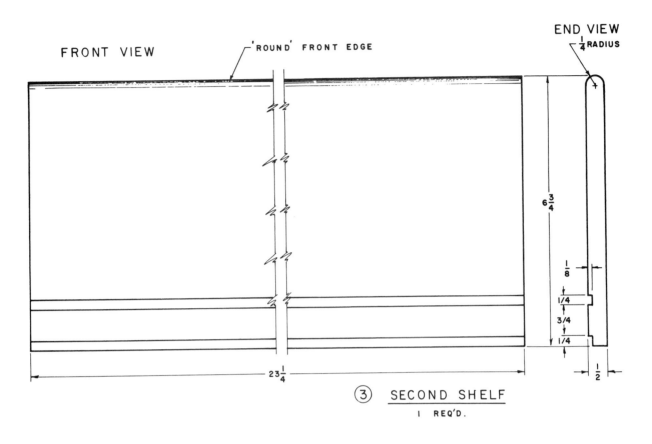

FRONT VIEW

'ROUND' FRONT EDGE

END VIEW
$\frac{1}{4}$ RADIUS

$6\frac{3}{4}$

$\frac{1}{8}$

1/4

3/4

1/4

$23\frac{1}{4}$

$\frac{1}{2}$

③ SECOND SHELF
1 REQ'D.

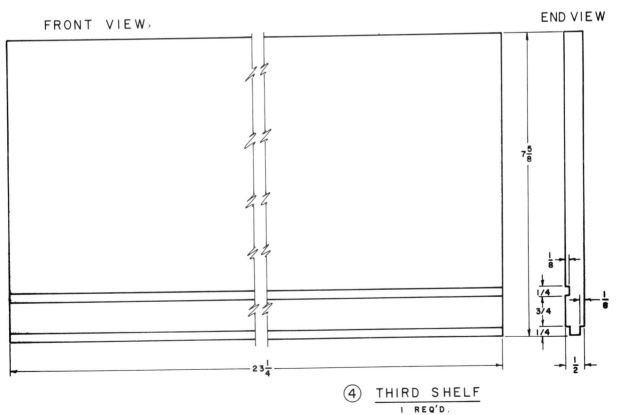

FRONT VIEW,

END VIEW

$7\frac{5}{8}$

$\frac{1}{8}$

1/4

$\frac{1}{8}$

3/4

1/4

$23\frac{1}{4}$

$\frac{1}{2}$

④ THIRD SHELF
1 REQ'D.

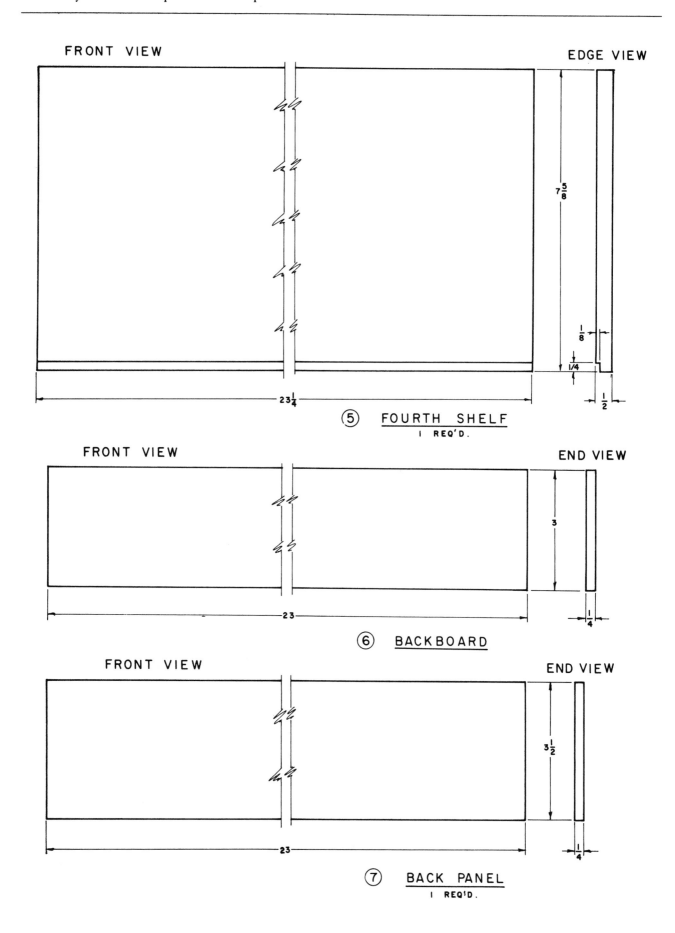

FRONT VIEW   EDGE VIEW

$7\frac{5}{8}$

$\frac{1}{8}$

1/4

23$\frac{1}{4}$

$\frac{1}{2}$

(5)   FOURTH SHELF

1 REQ'D.

FRONT VIEW   END VIEW

3

23

$\frac{1}{4}$

(6)   BACKBOARD

FRONT VIEW   END VIEW

$3\frac{1}{2}$

23

$\frac{1}{4}$

(7)   BACK PANEL

1 REQ'D.

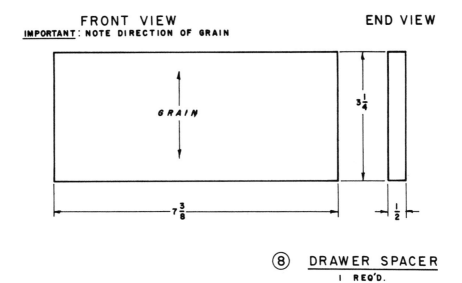

FRONT VIEW
IMPORTANT: NOTE DIRECTION OF GRAIN

END VIEW

GRAIN

$3\frac{1}{4}$

$7\frac{3}{8}$

$\frac{1}{2}$

⑧ DRAWER SPACER
1 REQ'D.

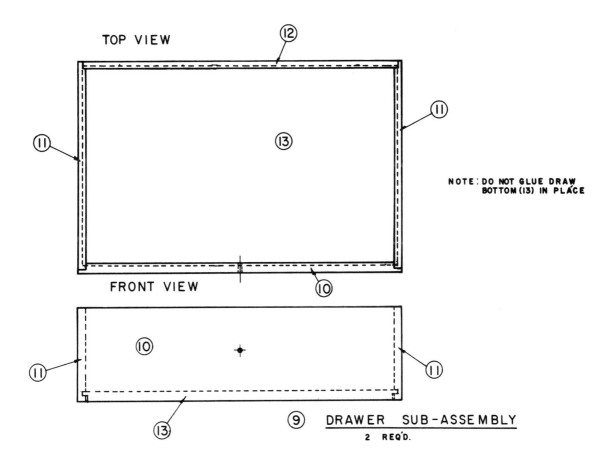

TOP VIEW

NOTE: DO NOT GLUE DRAW
BOTTOM (13) IN PLACE

FRONT VIEW

⑨ DRAWER SUB-ASSEMBLY
2 REQ'D.

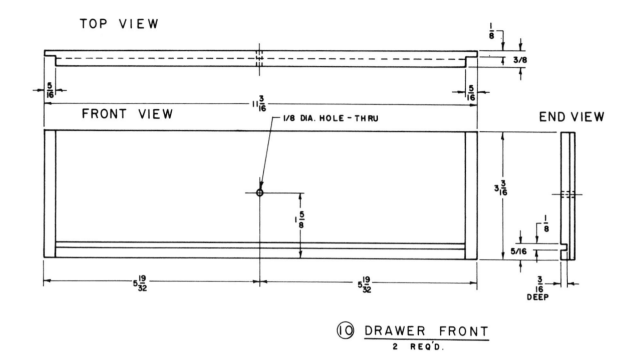

TOP VIEW

FRONT VIEW

END VIEW

1/8 DIA. HOLE – THRU

⑩ DRAWER FRONT
2 REQ'D.

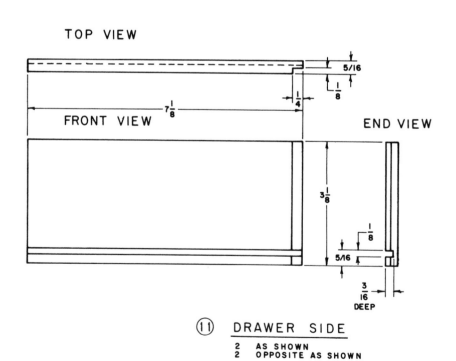

TOP VIEW

FRONT VIEW

END VIEW

⑪ DRAWER SIDE
2   AS SHOWN
2   OPPOSITE AS SHOWN

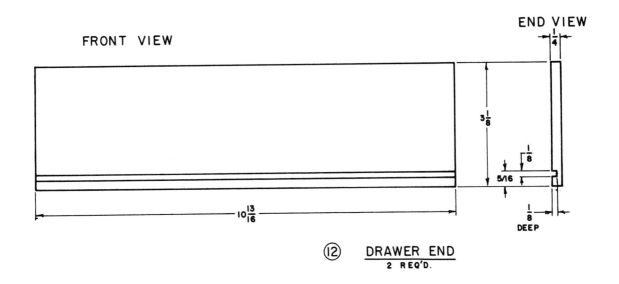

FRONT VIEW

END VIEW

$3\frac{1}{8}$

$\frac{1}{4}$

$\frac{1}{8}$

5/16

$10\frac{13}{16}$

$\frac{1}{8}$
DEEP

⑫   DRAWER END
2 REQ'D.

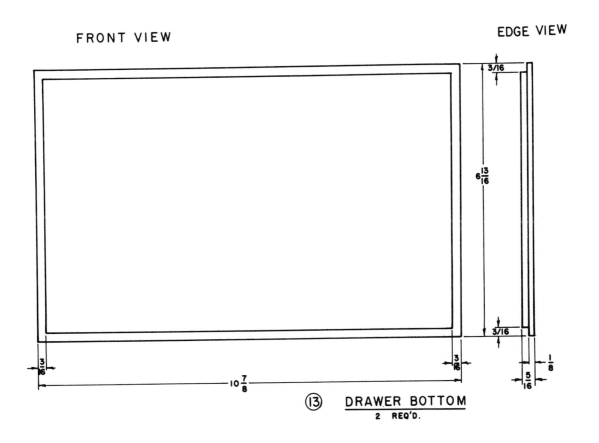

FRONT VIEW

EDGE VIEW

3/16

$6\frac{13}{16}$

3/16

$\frac{3}{16}$

$\frac{3}{16}$

$10\frac{7}{8}$

$\frac{1}{8}$

$\frac{5}{16}$

⑬   DRAWER BOTTOM
2 REQ'D.

Heirloom Watch Stand

Almost everyone has an old family watch packed away and forgotten in some drawer. This project will give you a chance to get that family heirloom out of its hiding place and displayed in the middle of your living room. It will also give you a chance to try your hand at a simple dovetail joint. A lathe (or a friend with a lathe!) would be helpful, but not necessary.

MATERIAL

1 ¼- by 10-inch by 2-foot #2 pine board
1 ½- by 3- by 6-inch #2 pine board
2 1-inch-diameter by 3-inch-long lathe turnings (see detail drawing)
1 small eyebolt or hook (open eyebolt to use)
4 ¾-inch-diameter wooden drawer pulls
4 #8 screws, flat-head, ¾ inches long
Wood glue
Water putty
Sandpaper, medium and fine
Steel wool, #0000 grade
Stain of your choice
Tung oil

CONSTRUCTION

Cut front panel (plan 1) to outside size 4¾ by 5½ inches. Locate and drill (or saw out) the watch face diameter. Check the diameter of your watch crystal and make this hole accordingly. Very carefully, measure and lay out the dovetails to exact size. Cut the dovetails along the inside of each cut. Use a chisel to remove the inside surface. Take your time. A dovetail must be nearly exact in order to ensure a tight fit.

Cut the two side panels (part 2) to outside size 2⅛ by 5½ inches. Measure and cut the dovetails according to the dimensions, as indicated on the detail drawing. It is a good idea to compare the cuts made in Part 1 before proceeding. Cut back panel (plan 3) to size 4½ by 5½ inches and carefully cut out the 3- by 4-inch rectangular hole.

Cut top support (part 5) and bottom support (part 6) to size and "round" the front and sides according to the detail drawing plans.

Cut arch (part 6) to size, 2½ by 6 inches, and lightly lay out the ¼-inch grid. Transfer the shape of the arch to the wood and cut. Take care when cutting the top section, as it is very weak. Drill two ⁵⁄₁₆-inch-diameter holes approximately ½-inch deep.

The two pillars (part 7) are turned by a lathe. If you do not have access to a lathe, try to locate commercially "turned" pillars approximately 1 inch in diameter by 3 inches long. If commercial turnings are not available, look for chair turnings approximately the cor-

rect size and cut to size. The photograph shows chair turnings cut to 3-inch lengths. This is not as good as the recommended turning (as illustrated in Part 7), but you will get by. The correct shape is dimensioned according to plan 7, but anything close to this will do.

Lay out the front trim (part 8) on a ¼-inch grid. The first step should be to locate and drill two ¼-inch-diameter holes as indicated in the detail plan. With a coping saw, cut out the profile. Sand the edges down to the pencil line.

Lay out the side trim (part 9) on a ¼-inch grid. As for part 8, locate and drill a ¼-inch diameter and cut to line. Be sure the two side trims are identical.

ASSEMBLY

Glue the front panel (part 1) to the two side panels (part 2) and the back panel (part 3). The dovetail joints should fit exactly. Sand to fit if necessary. After the glue sets, fill with wood putty and sand all four surfaces and top and bottom with a sanding block. Be sure to sand all corners sharp and "square."

Locate and glue the front trim (part 8), two side trims (part 9), and top support (part 5) in place. Glue top support (part 5), with top trim in place, to main body subassembly (parts 1, 2, and 3), and glue bottom support. Be sure to line up the back surfaces of these parts.

Fit and glue the two turnings (part 7) to the arch (part 6) and slip it in place between the top and bottom supports, as shown in the assembly drawing.

To make the four feet cut the end off the four wooden drawer pulls so they are approximately ½ inch long. Drill a hole through the center of each and countersink the bottom of each. Locate each, approximately as shown, and screw in place. Using your watch as a guide, locate an appropriate spot for the eyelet so that the watch hangs exactly centered in the hole provided for the crystal. A spacer may be needed. It will take a little time to locate the exact spot, so the watch is both centered and hanging free.

FINISHING

Stain to suit and add four or five coats of tung oil.

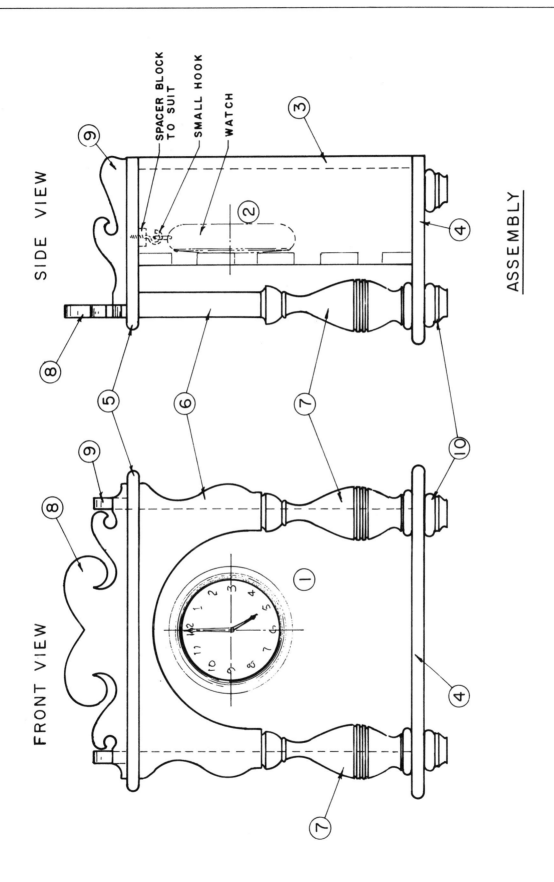

SIDE VIEW

SPACER BLOCK TO SUIT

SMALL HOOK

WATCH

FRONT VIEW

ASSEMBLY

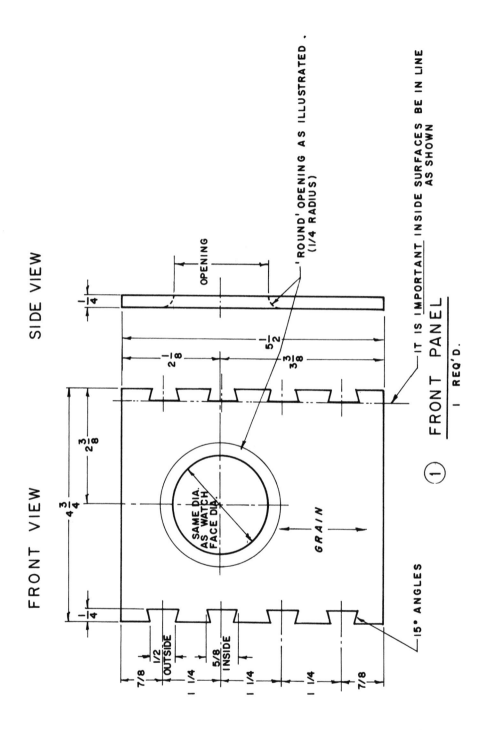

SIDE VIEW

FRONT VIEW

'ROUND' OPENING AS ILLUSTRATED .
(1/4 RADIUS)

IT IS IMPORTANT INSIDE SURFACES BE IN LINE
AS SHOWN

OPENING

FRONT PANEL

1 REQ'D.

SAME DIA.
AS WATCH
FACE DIA.

GRAIN

15° ANGLES

OUTSIDE

INSIDE

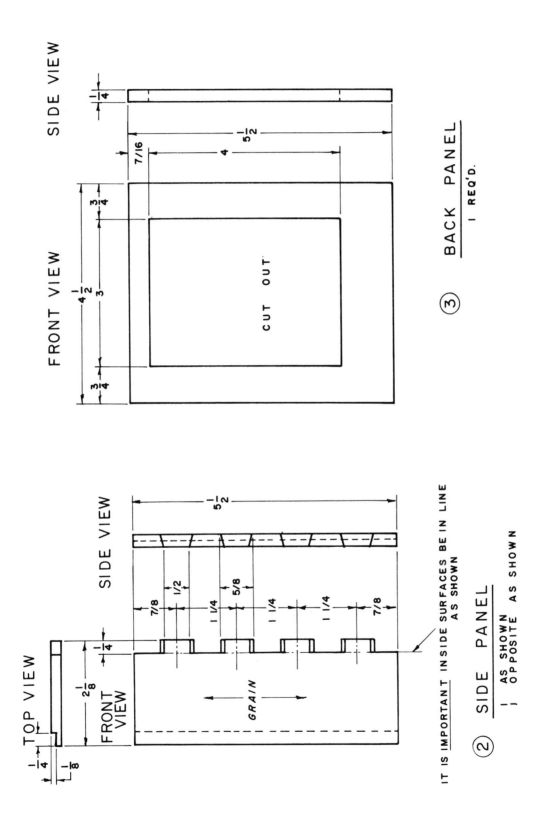

SIDE VIEW

FRONT VIEW

CUT OUT

③ BACK PANEL
1 REQ'D.

TOP VIEW

SIDE VIEW

FRONT VIEW

GRAIN

IT IS IMPORTANT INSIDE SURFACES BE IN LINE AS SHOWN

② SIDE PANEL
1 AS SHOWN
1 OPPOSITE AS SHOWN

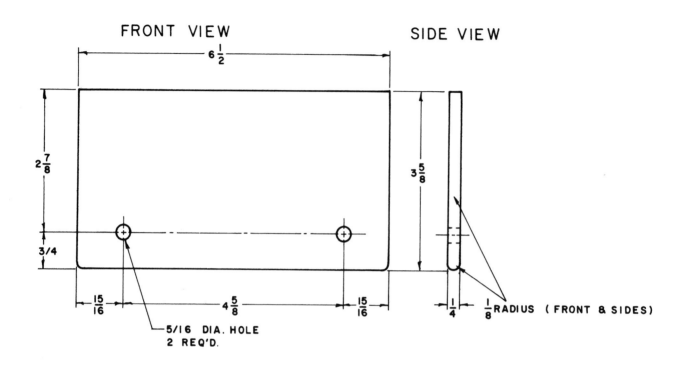

FRONT VIEW   SIDE VIEW

5/16 DIA. HOLE
2 REQ'D.

1/8 RADIUS (FRONT & SIDES)

④   BOTTOM SUPPORT
I   REQ'D.

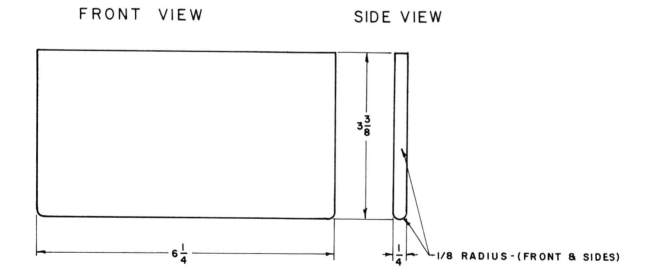

FRONT VIEW   SIDE VIEW

1/8 RADIUS - (FRONT & SIDES)

⑤   TOP SUPPORT
I   REQ'D.

FRONT VIEW   SIDE VIEW

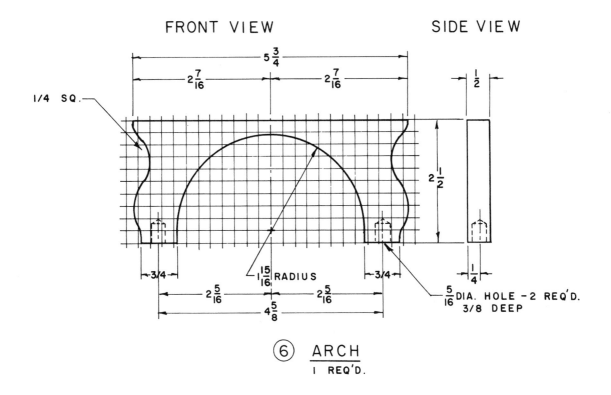

6 ARCH
1 REQ'D.

SIDE VIEW   END VIEW

NOTE: ANY TURNING 3" LONG OF THIS APPROX.
SHAPE COULD BE USED

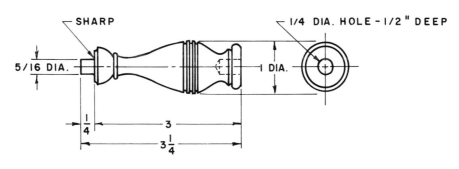

7 PILLAR
2 REQ'D.

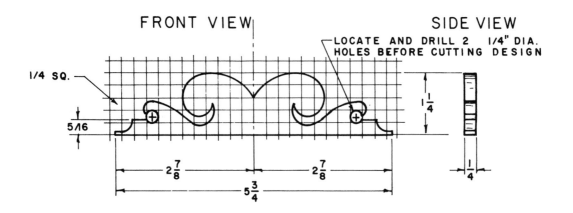

FRONT VIEW   SIDE VIEW

LOCATE AND DRILL 2 1/4" DIA.
HOLES BEFORE CUTTING DESIGN

1/4 SQ.

5/16

$1\frac{1}{4}$

$2\frac{7}{8}$ $2\frac{7}{8}$

$5\frac{3}{4}$

$\frac{1}{4}$

⑧ FRONT TRIM

I REQ'D.

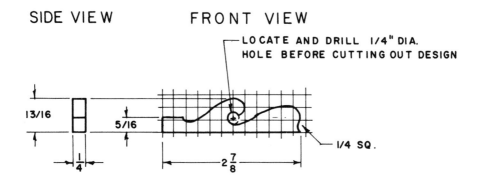

SIDE VIEW   FRONT VIEW

LOCATE AND DRILL 1/4" DIA.
HOLE BEFORE CUTTING OUT DESIGN

13/16

5/16

$\frac{1}{4}$

1/4 SQ.

$2\frac{7}{8}$

⑨ SIDE TRIM

2 REQ'D.

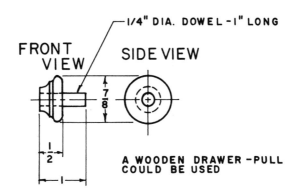

FRONT VIEW
SIDE VIEW

1/4" DIA. DOWEL – 1" LONG

$\frac{7}{8}$

$\frac{1}{2}$

1

A WOODEN DRAWER – PULL
COULD BE USED

⑩ FOOT
4 REQ'D.

Supplies

To make any antique project complete, the correct style, accessories, and fasteners, stain, and paint must be used. Some of the many suppliers that can furnish you with that special item you need to complete your new "antique" are listed below. This list is not complete, but should get you started. Many of these companies provide free catalogs of their products; others charge a nominal fee. Prices of their products vary also, so it does pay to compare both product and price.

The various publications listed are but a few of the many woodworking-related magazines. These publications are extremely helpful and provide many tips and ideas for working. Many will send a sample copy of their magazine for your review.

CATALOGS

Brookstone Co.
Vose Farm Road
Peterborough, NH 03458

Chaselle Arts and Crafts Inc.
9645 Gerwing Lane
Columbia, MD 21046

Constantine's
2050 Eastchester Road
Bronx, NY 10461

Craftsman Wood Service Co.
1735 West Cortland Court
Addison, IL 60101

The Fine Tool Shops
20 Backus Ave.
P.O. Box 1262
Danbury, CT 06810

Industrial Arts Supply Co.
5724 West Thirty-sixth St.
Minneapolis, MN 55416

International Home Library
14439 N. Seventy-third St.
Scottsdale, AZ 85260

Leichtung Inc.
4944 Commerce Pkwy.
Cleveland, OH 44128

Nasco Arts and Crafts
901 Janesville Ave.
Atkinson, WI 53538

Pyramid Artists Materials
Box 27
Urbana, IL 61801

Sax Arts and Crafts
P.O. Box 2002
Milwaukee, WI 53201

Silvo Hardware Co.
2205 Richmond St.
Philadelphia, PA 19125

Trendlines
375 Beacham St.
Chelsea, MA 02150

Woodcraft
41 Atlantic Ave.
P.O. Box 4000
Woburn, MA 01888

The Woodworkers Store
21801 Industrial Blvd.
Rogers, MN 55374

CLOCK SUPPLIES

Craft Products Co.
Dept. 14
2200 Dean St.
St. Charles, IL 60174

H. DeCounick & Son
200 Market Plaza
P.O. Box 68
Alamo, CA 94507

Emperor Clock Co.
Dept. 435
Emperor Industrial Park
Fairhope, AL 36532

Empire Clock Co.
1295 Rice St.
St. Paul, MN 55117

S. LaRose Inc.
234 Commerce Place
Greensboro, NC 27420

Mason & Sullivan Co.
586 Higgins Crowell Rd.
West Yarmouth
Cape Cod, MA 02678

Merritt's Antiques Inc.
RD 2
Douglassville, PA 19518

FINISHING PRODUCTS

Cohassett Colonials
Cohassett, MA 02025

Deft Inc.
17452 Von Darman Ave.
Irvine, CA 92713-9507

Formby's Inc.
825 Crossover Lane, Suite 240
Memphis, TN 38117

General Finishers
P.O. Box 14363-F
Milwaukee, WI 53214

The Knight Corporation
Box 894
Memphis, TN 38101

The Old-Fashioned Milk Paint Co.
Main Street
Groton, MA 01450

Refinishing Products, Inc.
P.O. Box 788
Olive Branch, MS 38654

Stulb Paint and Chemical Co., Inc.
P.O. Box 297
Norristown, PA 19404

Watco-Dennis Corporation
Michigan Ave. & 22nd St.
Santa Monica, CA 90404

FURNITURE HARDWARE

The Brass Tree
308 N. Main St.
Charles, MO 63301

Charolette Ford Trunks
Box 536
Spearman, TX 74081

The Decorative Hardware Studio
160 King Street
Chappaqua, NY 10514

Garrett Wade Co., Inc.
161 Ave. of the Americas
New York, NY 10013

Heirloom Antiques Brass Co.
P.O. Box 146
Dundass, MN 55019

Horton Brasses
P.O. Box 95
Nooks Hill Road
Cromwell, CT 06416

Imported European Hardware
4295 S. Arville
Las Vegas, NV 89103

19th Century Hardware Supply Co.
P.O. Box 599
Rough and Ready, CA 95975

The Old Country Store
West Mansfield Village, MA 02083

Old Guilford Forge
1840 Boston Post Road
Guilford, CT 06437

Paxton
Upper Falls, MD 21156

The Renovator's Supply
Miller's Falls, MA 01349

Ritter & Son Hardware
Dept. WJ
Gualala, CA 95445

Samuel Cabot Inc.
One Union Street
Boston, MA 02108

Tech-Ni-Craft
Box 217
Auburn, MA 01501

The Wise Co.
6503 St. Claude Ave.
Arabi, LA 70032

The Woodworkers Store
21801 Industrial Blvd.
Rogers, MN 55374

OLD-FASHIONED NAILS

Equality Screw Co., Inc.
P.O. Box 1296
El Cajon, CA 92002

Tremont Nail Co.
21 Elm St.
P.O. Box 111
Wareham, MA 02571

SPECIAL WOOD STOCK

Austin Hardwoods
2119 Goodrich
Austin, TX 78701

Beauty-Wood Industries
91 Eglington Ave. E.
Mississauga, Ontario
Canada

Maurice L. Condon Co., Inc.
248 Ferris Ave.
White Plains, NY 10603

Constantine's
2050 Eastchester Rd.
Bronx, NY 10461

Educational Lumber Co.
P.O. Box 5373
Asheville, NC 28813

Bob Morgan Woodworking Supplies
1123 Bardstown Rd.
Louisville, KY 40204

The Sawmill
P.O. Box 329
Nazareth, PA 18064

Unicorn Universal Woods Ltd.
137 John Street.
Toronto, Canada M5V-2E4

Wood World
9006 Waukegan Road
Morton Grove, IL 60053

Woods of the World Inc.
Route 202
P.O. Box 112
Antrim, NH 03440

STENCILING SUPPLIES

Adelle Bishop Inc.
Dorset, VT 05251

WOODWORKING TOOLS

Armor Products
P.O. Box 290
Deer Park, NY 11729

Ball and Ball
463 W. Lincoln Hgwy.
Exton, PA 19341

Brookstone Co.
Vose Farm Road
Peterborough, NH 03458

Conover Woodcraft Specialties
18124 Madison Rd.
Parkman, OH 44080

Frog Tool Co. Ltd.
700 W. Jackson Blvd.
Dept. 5E
Chicago, IL 60606

Greenlee Tool Division
2330 Twenty-third Ave.
Rockford, IL 61101

The Toolroom
East Oxbow Rd. (780 FW)
Shelburne Falls, MA 01370

U.S. General Supply Corp.
Dept. A-309
100 General Place
Jericho, NY 11753

RELATED PUBLICATIONS (MAGAZINES)

The American Woodworker
JM Publications Inc.
13 Walton Mall Box 1408
Hendersonville, TN 37075

Early American Life
P.O. Box 8200
Harrisburg, PA 17105

Fine Woodworking
The Taunton Press
52 Church Hill Rd. Box 355
Newton, CT 06470

Hands On
6640 Poe Ave.
Dayton, OH 45414-2591

International Woodworking Magazine
Plymouth, NH 03264

Popular Woodworker
EGW Publishing Co.
1300 Galaxy Way
Concord, CA 94520

Wood
Box 10625
Des Moines, IA 50380-0625

Woodsmith
2200 Grand Ave.
Des Moines, IA 50312

The Woodworker's Journal
517 Litchfield Rd.
P.O. Box 1629
New Milford, CT 06776

Workbench Magazine
Box 5965
Kansas City, MO 64110

RELATED PUBLICATIONS (BOOKS)

Hammond, James, et al. *Woodworking Technology.* Illinois: McKnight Publishing Co., 1980.
Margon, Lester. *Construction of American Furniture Treasures.* New York: Dover Publications, Inc., 1975.
Nye, Alvan Crocker. *American Colonial Furniture in Scaled Drawings.* New York: Dover Publications, Inc., 1982.
Osburn, Burl N., and Osburn, Bernice B. *Measured Drawings of Early American Furniture.* New York: Dover Publications, Inc., 1974.
Russell, Robert B. *Attractive and Easy-to-Build Wood Projects.* New York: Dover Publications, Inc., 1980.
Shea, John G. *Colonial Furniture Making for Everybody.* New York: Van Nostrand Reinhold Co., 1964.
Stickley, Gustav. *Making Authentic Craftsman Furniture: Instructions and Plans for 50 Projects.* New York: Dover Publications, Inc., 1985.
Villard, Paul. *A Manual of Veneering.* New York: Dover Publications, Inc., 1974.
Waring, Janet. *Early American Stencils on Walls and Furniture.* New York: Dover Publications, Inc., 1968.
Watson, Aldren A. *Country Furniture.* New York: Thomas Y. Crowell Co., 1974.

WOODWORKING ASSOCIATIONS, CLUBS AND GUILDS

Alabama Woodworkers Guild
P.O. Box 327
Pelham, AL 35214

Alaska Creative Woodworkers
Greg Motyka
2136 Alder Dr.
Anchorage, AK 99508

Augusta Woodworkers Guild
Box 15 Augusta, MO 63332

Baulines Craftsman Guild
55 Sunnyside
Mill Valley, CA 94941

Green Country Woodworkers Club
P.O. Box 470856
Tulsa, OK 74147-0856

Guild of Oregon Woodworkers
P.O. Box 1866
Portland, OR 97207

Inland Empire Woodworkers Guild
P.O. Box 7413
Spokane, WA 99207-0413

Kansas City Woodworkers Guild
510 N. Sterling
Sugar Creek, MO 64054

Michigan Woodworkers Guild
P.O. Box 7802
Ann Arbor, MI 48107

Midwest Woodworkers Association
Gerald Jones
311 Cumberland Rd.
Columbia, MO 65203

North Texas Woodworkers Guild
P.O. Box 224886
Dallas, TX 75222

Society of Philadelphia Woodworkers
% Chestnut Hill Academy
500 W. Willow Grove Ave.
Philadelphia, PA 19118

Souris Valley Woodworkers Assn.
P.O. Box 3042
Minot, ND 58702

Southeast American Craft Council
Art Department
Longwood College
Farmville, VA 23901

Vancouver Island Woodworkers Guild
Box 6584, Station C
Victoria, British Columbia
Canada V8P 5N7

Virginia Mountain Crafts Guild
P.O. Box 1001
Salem, VA 24153

Wisconsin Woodworkers Guild
Jim Lingle, President
P.O. Box 137
Milwaukee, WS 53201

Woodworkers Association of North America
P.O. Box 706
Plymouth, NH 03264

Woodworkers Association of Topeka
Cleo McDonald, President
9421 N.W. Forty-second St.
Silver Lake, KS 66539

Woodworkers Guild of Georgia
Box 1113
Conyers, GA 30207

The Woodwrights Gallery
Box 7571
Klamath Falls, OR 97602

MAJOR HISTORICAL COLLECTIONS OF EARLY AMERICAN FURNITURE

Clock Museum
Bristol, CT 06010

Colonial Williamsburg
Williamsburg, VA 23185

Farmer's Museum
Cooperstown, NY 13326

Greenfield Village
Dearborn, MI 48100

Maritime Museum
San Francisco, CA 94100

Shelburne Museum
Route 7
Shelburne, VT 05401

Index

Accessories, 7
Adjustable candle stand, 94–101
Antique-cut nails, 7, 124
Ash, 6
Assembly drawings, 12, 13

Balloons, 13
Basswood, 6
Bench, Pennsylvania Dutch child's,
    70–77
Birch, 6
Bit brace, 8
Blanket chest, six-board, 78–85
Block, sanding, 9
Books, related, 125
Book shelf, hanging, with drawers,
    102–111
Butternut, 6

Candle box, "lollipop," 36–41
Candleholder, Shaker, 20–25
Candle stand, adjustable, 94–101
Catalogs, 7, 122
Character of wood, 6, 11
Chest, six-board blanket, 78–85
Cherry, 6
Chestnut, 6
Child's bench, Pennsylvania Dutch,
    70–77
Chippendale mirror frame, 48–53
Chisel, wood, 9
Clamp, wood, 9
Claw hammer, 9
Clock supplies, 123
Colonial style, 11
Common lumber, 6
Coping saw, 9
Cross-cut saw, 8
Cupboard, standing, 86–93

Density of wood, 6
Detail drawings, 12, 15
Distressing process, 11, 16
Drill, electric, 10
Drill press, 10
Drying rack, Shaker, 42–47

Early American furniture, 5, 126
Eastern white pine, 6
Eighteenth-century pipe holder, 60–69
Electric drill, 10
Elm, 6
Evergreen trees, 6

Federal style, 11

Finishing process, 12–16
Finishing products, 123
Footstool, eighteenth-century, 14–19
Furniture hardware, 123

Gluing instructions, 11
Grades of wood, 6
Gum wood, 6

Half-round rasp, 11
Hammer, 8
Hanging book shelf with drawers,
    102–111
Hardware, furniture, 123
Hardwood, 6
Heirloom watch stand, 112–121

Instructions, 6, 11

Jack plane, 9

Limba wood, 6
"Lollipop" candle box, 36–41
Lumber, common, 6
Lumber size, 7

Magazines, related, 125
Mahogany, 6
Maple, 6
Medium wood, 6
Milk paint, 13, 123
Mirror frame, Chippendale, 48–53
Multi-view drawing system, 12–13
Museums, 126

Nail set, 8
Nails, antique-cut, 7, 124
Northern pitch pine, 6

Oak wood, 6
Old-fashioned nails, 124
Open-grained wood, 6

Periods of styles, 11
Pennsylvania Dutch child's bench,
    70–77
Pilgrim style, 11
Pipe holder, eighteenth-century, 60–69
Pine wood, 6
Plane-jack, 8
Popular wood, 6
Publications, books, 125
Publications, magazines, 125
"Pumpkin" pine, 6

Radial-arm saw, 10

Rasp, half-round, 11
Red cedar wood, 6
Red pine wood, 6
Redwood wood, 6
Router, 10

Saber saw, 10
Sander, electric, 10
Sanding block, 9
Saw, coping, 9
Saw, radial-arm, 10
Saw, table, 10
Saw, saber, 10
Screw, brass, 123
Screwdriver, 10
Set, nail, 8
Shave, spoke, 10
Shaker drying rack, 42–47
Silverware tray, 30–35
Six-board blanket chest, 78–85
Softwood, 6
Southern hard pine, 6
Special wood stock, 124
Spoke shave, 10
Square, try, 8
Standing cupboard, 86–93
Steel wool, 11
Stenciling supplies, 124
Style, 5
Supplies, 122

Tape measure, 7
Three-rail towel rack, 26–29
Three-shelf wall rack, 54–59
Tool supplies, 124
Tray, silverware, 30–35
Try square, 8
Tung oil, 13

Vendors, 7, 122

Wall rack, three-shelf, 54–59
Walnut wood, 6
Wash coat, 13
Watch stand, heirloom, 112–121
White pine wood, 61
Willow wood, 6
Wood clamps, 9
Wood classifications, 6
Wood chisels, 9
Wood supplies, 124
Woodworking Associations,
    Clubs and Guilds, 125

Yellow pine, 6